Mergers, Acquisitions, and Divestitures

A Guide to Their Impact for Investors and Directors

Mergers, Acquisitions, and Divestitures

A Guide to Their Impact for Investors and Directors

Thomas Hollis Hopkins
Principal
The Vail Consultancy
Vail, Colorado

DOW JONES-IRWIN
Homewood, Illinois 60430

©THOMAS HOLLIS HOPKINS, 1983

All rights reserved. No part of this publication may be reproduced, stored in a retrieval system, or transmitted, in any form or by any means, electronic, mechanical, photocopying, recording, or otherwise, without the prior written permission of the copyright holder.

This publication is designed to provide accurate and authoritative information in regard to the subject matter covered. It is sold with the understanding that the publisher is not engaged in rendering legal, accounting, or other professional service. If legal advice or other expert assistance is required, the services of a competent professional person should be sought.

From a Declaration of Principles jointly adopted by a Committee of the American Bar Association and a Committee of Publishers.

ISBN 0-87094-200-X

Library of Congress Catalog Card No. 82-71347

Printed in the United States of America

1 2 3 4 5 6 7 8 9 0 K 0 9 8 7 6 5 4 3

To Harry and Joan Hopkins

This book is dedicated to my parents. Most people feel gratitude toward their parents, but few could feel it as acutely as I do. Their values, attitudes, examples, sacrifices, and successes have provided the foundation and much of the inspiration for my life. They deserve such regard, entirely. I am most thankful to them both.

There is another person in my life for whom I am very thankful. My wife, Pam, is a very positive influence and loving support. Her encouragement and her serenity have enabled much in my life to come into perspective and to fruition. Thank you Pam.

Preface

The value of a company, and hence the wealth of its shareholders, can be affected dramatically by its acquisition of another company or its decision to sell. Perhaps no other decision can have as swift and significant an impact on a company's value. This book focuses on that impact. It considers the specific effects of the buy, sell, and spin-off decisions, and it discusses how a company can develop an acquisition or divestiture strategy which will have a positive impact on its value.

Three groups of people are critically interested in the impact of an acquisition or divestiture on a company's value. First, the investor who is a shareholder of the company or who could become one. The impact on his economic well-being can be significant, and he can influence a company's activities through collective action with other investors. Second, the security analyst whose function is to ascertain the impact of the various decisions and strategies, and to make buy/sell recommendations to the investment community. Third, the director of a company who has a fiduciary responsibility to the shareholders. He must approve a major acquisition or sale, and he can influence a company towards a positive strategy. To these people this book is directed.

Thomas Hollis Hopkins

Contents

Section One   A Conceptual Framework, 1
The Stand-Alone Value of a Company, 4
Value-Added in a Merger, 10
   Operational Benefits, 11
   Nonoperational Benefits, 16
   Costs, 25

Section Two   Acquiring Companies, 31
The Buy Decision Point, 33
Buy Strategy 1—The Pursuit of Value-Added, 37
   Horizontal Acquisitions, 37
   Conglomerate Acquisitions, 40
   Vertical Acquisitions, 43
   Value-Added and Relatedness, 43
   Strengths and Weaknesses, 46
   Joint Ventures, 47
Buy Strategy 2—The Pursuit of Bargains, 48
Diversifying Successfully, 53
Empirical Evidence, 56
   Study 1—Multiple Classifications, 57
   Study 2—Conglomerates, 61

Section Three   Selling, Divesting, and Spinning-Off Companies, 65
The Sell Decision Point, 67
Sell Strategies, 70
Spinning-Off Businesses, 79

Section Four   The Evaluation of a Merger, 85
Du Pont's Purchase of Conoco, 87
  A Du Pont Director, 89
  A Conoco Director, 99
  A Security Analyst, 102
  The Conoco Shareholders, 105
  The Du Pont Shareholders, 105
Conclusions, 107
  Buyers, 107
  Sellers, 109

Postscript: A Broader Perspective, 111
Society's Interests, 113
The Decision Criteria Revisited, 119
  The Buy Situation, 119
  The Sell Situation, 120
  The Spin-Off Situation, 121

Notes, 123

Index, 133

Section One

A Conceptual Framework

It is possible to combine two companies and to rationalize their operations so that the resulting company is thereby better able to produce the goods and services that society desires. Society will benefit.

And society will reward such a combination. Society will increase the market value of the combined company above that of the component companies by an amount which reflects the improved ability to satisfy profitably society's needs.

The value of such a combined company is the stand-alone value of each component company, plus the value-added. Therefore, the ceiling price that should be paid for a company being considered for purchase is its stand-alone value plus the full amount of the value-added. The buyer would need to pay less than this if its shareholders are to gain and share in the extra value created. If the stand-alone value of a selling company is $30 million and the value-added with a buyer is $15 million, then the ceiling price that the buyer should pay is $45 million. If $40 million is paid, then the buying shareholders are ahead and their shares should be expected to rise in value. If too much is paid—say $50 million—then the market value of the buying shareholder's shares should be expected to drop.

Thus, when one company is considering buying or selling to another, two things should be known: first, the market value of the selling company, and how accurately this measures its underlying value; and second, the favorable interaction that will result from combining the two companies and hence the value-added that will result.

The Stand-Alone Value of a Company

The market value of a company is usually defined as the total value of all the outstanding debt and equity securities. For our purpose we need consider only the equity securities. Thus, if there are 1 million shares outstanding valued at $30 per share, we will define the market value as $30 million.

A key question is how accurately the company's shares are valued by its market. If the shares are undervalued, then there is a good chance of buying the company at a bargain price; if the shares are overvalued, then the company could be sold at a bonus price, one that is higher than normal.

The price of a company's shares will be correct at any moment if the market for those particular shares has three attributes: it knows all information about the company; it acts on that information instantly; and it is accurate in its assessment of the true import of the information. No company enjoys such a perfect market for its shares, but some come close, and these companies offer little chance of being bought at a bargain price and have less chance than others of selling at a bonus price. On the other hand, the market for some companies' shares does not nearly approach such perfection, and it is much more likely that these companies could be bought for a bargain or sold at a bonus.

Much may be known about the general characteristics of the exchange on which a company's shares are traded. But this is not enough. It is necessary to know just how good the market is for a particular company's shares. We can judge how good the market for a particular share is by examining those factors which determine the market's ability to act. The first set of factors is unique to the company or its industry.

Information policy. Some companies, as a matter of policy, are very secretive about their affairs and will provide the markets only the bare minimum of information that is required by law. On the other hand, some companies have the opposite policy of telling all. Recognizing that a stock market needs information to assess a company's prospects, it is clear that the market for the more open company's shares will be more accurate than that for a secretive company's shares. G. D. Searle & Co., the U.S. pharmaceutical firm, was very tight-lipped with the public during the early 1970s. Under a new chief executive officer, Mr. Donald Rumsfeld, Searle changed its policy, reportedly when it came to perceive that its shares were under-valued and that candor was one way to gain a more reasonable market valuation. G. D. Searle could well have been a bargain acquisition in the early 1970s.

External information. Irrespective of whether a company discusses its own prospects or not, the market can obtain insight into its future through external sources. An Australian company, Poseidon, discovered nickel in South Australia and its share price skyrocketed. A nearby company also discovered comparable amounts of nickel shortly thereafter. The announcement of this second find made very little impact on its share price, much to the disgust of some speculators who had bought on inside information. The explanation for this is that the local newspapers had published much speculation as to which way the ore body ran, and the stock market had fully anticipated that the second company would indeed find nickel. Its shares had already risen to a premium price at the time of the announcement. In fact, the share price actually fell within days of the announcement, because the market apparently anticipated more than was announced. Some industries are followed more closely than others, and the market values of companies in these industries are more accurate due to the greater quantity of external information.

Multibusinesses. When a company is made up of many separate and different businesses the market will have an obvious problem in valuing the total combination, largely due to a lack of information about each part. Hence, the total market value for such a company is unlikely to reflect accurately the total prospects for that company. The company should expect to be undervalued because such ignorance would constitute a risk in the eyes of the stock market which would then discount the company's shares.

Popularity. At any one time certain concepts can be in vogue that result in the over- or undervaluation of a particular company. For example, in the United States during the mid 1970s companies which were "stars" (having the greatest market share in a high growth market) were popular and could well have been overvalued; they could have been sold at a bonus price. On the other hand, companies which were "dogs" (having a small market share in a slow growth market) were out of vogue, and businessmen were advised to divest themselves of such businesses. These businesses were probably undervalued, below their real value at this time, and represented bargains. The same observation could apply to whole industries. Some are currently popular; some are not. High technology stocks were in vogue in the early 1980s. Their shares were probably overvalued at this time.

Shareholder following. Different companies appeal to different groups of shareholders and the sophistication of that group of shareholders will affect the accuracy with which the share price reflects the real prospects of the company. Companies which attract institutional buyers, buyers who are competing with one another to achieve the most favorable return on their respective portfolios, would tend to have accurate markets for their shares because they are backed with careful research. Other companies attract a strong following of less sophisticated groups. In Malaysia the cement market is split equally between two companies. One company's stock is considered stable, even staid, while the other's is considered highly speculative and its share price is volatile. And yet they are in the same industry and a large percentage of their respective earnings comes from the one joint venture. One explanation that was offered for this situation was that the speculative company's shareholders are largely Chinese who seem to operate in the stock market as short-term gamblers, and who have little interest in the underlying economic realities of a share's value. Analyzing a company's shareholders can say much about its current share price.

Trading activity. When a company's stock is actively traded, its value at any one time is more likely to be an accurate estimate of its true value than if the company is inactively traded and its market thin. Thus, a thin market for a security could well indicate an inaccurate market valuation and the possibility of obtaining a bargain or a bonus.

The second group of factors which determines the accuracy of a company's share price refers to the stock market on which the company is traded and the country within which that market is located. These factors include:

Market size. It is reasonable to expect that small regional markets would be less sophisticated than large national markets. For example, the New York Stock Exchange (NYSE), a national market, is more sophisticated than one of the regional American exchanges. Companies traded on the NYSE are probably valued more accurately than those on the smaller exchanges.

Country development. The more developed the country, the more likely that rational financial institutions will play a part, and the more sophisticated the stock market. We would expect the London market to reflect the prospects of a company more accurately than would the Indonesian market which was started in 1977 and which had only two companies listed as of 1979.

Customs. Different countries have different customs which can affect the sophistication of the stock markets. Countries whose economic life is dominated by a few individuals or families, or where bribery is normal conduct, are less likely to have a public stock market which accurately reflects a company's true economic worth.

A comparative study of the average degree of sophistication of different stock markets around the world has been done by comparing one variable, the speed of response to favorable information.[1] The study examined how quickly the share prices in a particular market rose with the public announcement of favorable information. The studies ranked the stock markets from the most sophisticated—Class I—through to the least sophisticated—Class III. The results were as follows:

Class I: With these markets the share price moved up before the favorable public announcement, in anticipation of the good news. This would indicate that the market acts on external information, but it could also result from insider trading. Markets exhibiting these characteristics are the New York, London, and Tokyo exchanges.

Class II: These markets do not generally anticipate public information but react very quickly to it, and security prices rise immediately upon the public announcement. This would indicate that there is little external analysis or insider trading which would permit anticipation of the good news. Markets exhibiting these characteristics are the Sydney and Melbourne stock exchanges.

Class III: These markets are slow to respond to information, often lagging behind the public anouncement by many months. Such a market could demonstrate a lack of sophistication on the part of investors, or various structural problems, which would cause a slow response. The Calcutta market is an example of this type market.

The results are presented graphically in Exhibit 1.

These results indicate that stock markets vary in their sophistication from the most sophisticated Class I markets in the large developed countries down to the least sophisticated Class III markets in underdeveloped countries.

Considerable evidence has been gathered on the Class I New York Stock Exchange.[2] The evidence shows that even this most sophisticated of markets is some way from the perfect market in which security prices reflect all of the information, instantly, and accu-

Exhibit 1

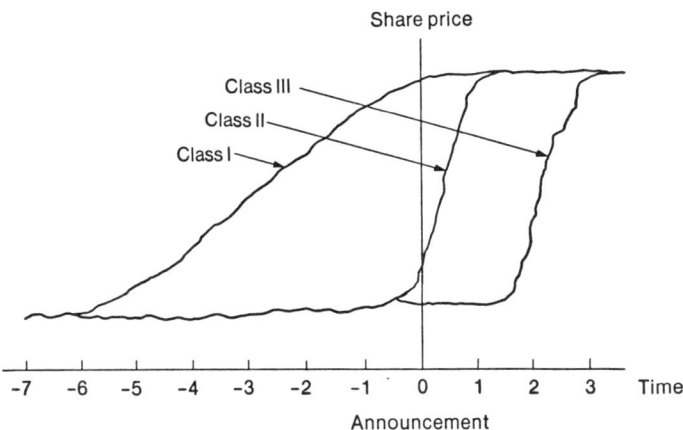

rately. The evidence shows that on average the security prices reflect at least all of the *public* information, rapidly and sometimes with anticipation, and fairly realistically. However, the point is that even with stocks traded on the New York Stock Exchange there is a possibility of finding particular companies which are over- or under-valued, and this possibility clearly increases as we move from companies traded on Class I markets through to those traded on Class III markets.

Thus, in assessing whether the stand-alone market value of a particular company is an accurate measure of its real value, it is necessary to think in terms of the company, its industry, and the stock market on which it is traded.

Value-Added in a Merger

The second factor in determining postmerger worth is the value-added, the value that the market places on the improved ability of the combined company to produce profitably the goods and services that society demands. The value-added equals the benefits less the costs that result from combining the two companies.

Operational Benefits

The first set of benefits is operational in nature:

1. Sales and marketing. By combining two companies it is possible to enhance the competitive market position by improving the market coverage, improving the distribution network, making the product line more complete, and improving market research. The PIMS (Profit Impact of Market Strategy) study by The Strategic Planning Institute indicates that there are distinct advantages in being large in a particular market place.[3] These include the ability to charge higher prices for a better-known product, and the freedom to maintain the price at an optimal level.

The Oasis chain of restaurants was acquired by Howard Johnson, a chain of motel/restaurants in the United States. The Oasis chain operated a series of restaurants built on bridgelike structures across the interstate highways in the Chicago area. By selling to Howard Johnson, a twofold marketing benefit was achieved; people would be more likely to stop at the restaurants because the Howard Johnson name was better known to interstate travellers, and they would be more likely to stay at a Howard Johnson's motel as a result of being reminded frequently of the name as they drove under each restaurant. Thus the Oasis restaurants were worth more as a part of Howard Johnson, due to the value-added, than as a stand-alone entity.

Admittedly, not all possible sales and marketing benefits are desirable from society's viewpoint. Some benefits can accrue to shareholders which are a cost to society as a whole. A company could buy out all of its competitors and thereby achieve a monopoly position that would permit excess profits, at least in the short-term. Or a company could acquire a safe base in another industry that would enable it to indulge in predatory pricing in its own. These possibilities will be discussed more fully in the Postscript.

2. **Costs and production.** These benefits result from lowering the cost of production by achieving economies of scale or other direct efficiencies, a classic justification for mergers. These advantages can be due to purchasing power, thus forcing suppliers to take lower prices, quantity discounts for bulk purchases, a source of low-cost feed stocks, the ability to write off fixed expenses over a greater number of units, the ability to reduce costs with greater cumulative experience. The PIMS study of over 2,000 different businesses in the United States indicated that cost reductions were a major advantage of size, and that purchases as a percent of sales declined from 45 percent on average for smaller companies to 33 percent for the largest companies.[4] This is one reason often cited to explain why General Motors is more profitable than Ford or Chrysler. The larger the product run, the lower the cost per unit.

3. **Research and technology.** These benefits result from a complementing of research or technological expertise and can result in greater sales, lower costs, improved resource utilization and so forth. It was the pursuit of these benefits that prompted Motorola Inc. to

acquire Codex Corporation for more than $80 million, a high price for a company earning some $3 million per year, and more than three times Codex's preoffer market value. The rationale given was that Codex possessed a device that allowed computer data to be transmitted over telephone lines and whose technology could be used throughout the Motorola product line. Codex would be more valuable as a part of Motorola than as a stand-alone company.

4. Resource. This benefit results from the better utilization of physical, human, and other resources. Scott Paper acquired Hollingsworth & Whitney, and one of the justifications given for this was that Hollingsworth's stands of timber in Maine were more suitable for the manufacture of the papers that Scott produced than those that Hollingsworth produced. These stands of timber were worth more when a part of Scott than when a part of just Hollingsworth.

Another form of this resource benefit is exhibited by a cyclical business when it acquires a countercyclical business and can thereby better utilize its resources during down times. The business it acquires is unique: it must have a different demand cycle but use the same resources. If a manufacturer of luxury recreational vehicles, a cyclical business which does poorly in bad times, were to acquire a manufacturer of cheap mobile homes, a countercyclical business which tends to do well in bad times, then it could better utilize its plants and people during down times by switching from the manufacture of recreational vehicles to the manufacture of mobile homes. Although the two products have opposite demand characteristics, they are basically the same product. One is a house bolted to a motor chassis and the other is a house towed to a site. They use the same resources. Fleetwood Enterprises is an example of a firm in this situation, making both recreational vehicles and mobile homes, although it achieved this situation by internal growth rather than by acquisition.

5. **Managerial.** This benefit results from the introduction of superior management skills, thereby creating a better company. The replacement of incompetent management by the competent is another classic justification for acquisitions. It is also the justification frequently given for the acquisition of a company by a successful, retired senior executive. A controlling interest in Crutcher Resources Corp., a manufacturer of automatic pipeline welding equipment much of which is sold to oil companies, was acquired by a group of investors who then installed Mr. J. Kenneth Jamieson as the chief executive officer. Presumably this would have added management benefits because Mr. Jamieson was the retired chairman of Exxon, the world's biggest oil company, and he could add much to the efficient operation of the company.

But how significant, how likely is this benefit? Can a competent top-level manager manage any business? Joel Dean and Winfield Smith in *The Corporate Merger* said:

> A good manager's 'intuitions,' like those of a good card player, come from his long experience with the special rules, technology, and markets of his particular industry; only in extraordinary individuals—so few in number as to be practically negligible—do we find the ability to absorb a new game intellectually and then compete successfully with experienced players.[5]

Dean and Smith were saying in effect that top-level strategic competence is industry specific.

How robust is their analogy? It surely depends on the nature of the industry. If the industry is dominated by a few companies which arrived there by successfully competing while lesser competitors were forced out, and which are still competing aggressively, then this is analogous to a very sophisticated game of "Bridge." A novice to such an industry would have little chance of success. On the other hand, in a highly fractured industry with many small competitors, or in an industry which has gone to sleep and which is no longer competing aggressively, or in a business which has come on hard times because of gross mismanagement, these situations are analogous to the rather simple game of "Fish," and a good manager could step in and create value just by introducing basic but good management techniques.

It also seems to be easier for individuals to move from industry to industry than for corporate bureaucracies. A bureaucracy develops an ability to operate effectively within one industry, but if it goes into a new industry, it seems to be less able to adapt than can an individual. It is possible to point to numerous examples of individual managers who have succeeded in one industry and then another but to fewer corporate bureaucracies.

The above five benefits are all operational in nature. They can be very significant and are at the heart of the merger process. It is easy to point to potential operational benefits when going into an acquisition situation; it is an entirely different matter to realize them. A large health care organization acquired a contract cleaning company in the early 1970s. One reason cited for the acquisition was that the large organization would provide the cleaner with an entree, via its supply division, to all North American hospitals. It sounded good, a marketing benefit. But it never happened. The contract cleaner was put into a different group from the supply division, and the supply division's sales people were never even aware of the contract cleaner. Further, the person in a hospital who procures supplies is not usually the one who purchases cleaning services. The contract cleaner was eventually sold off.

To achieve such benefits is usually a painful process. Sales forces must be rationalized and retrained, plants closed, employees laid off, research efforts redirected, management fired—a bloody affair. Any manager who sets out to do a gentlemanly acquisition, in which no such rationalization is attempted, is fooling himself if he is justifying the acquisition by the value-added that is to result.

Nonoperational Benefits

In addition to these operational benefits, it is possible to find nonoperational benefits, including the following:

1. Funding. By combining several companies into one larger company, it is possible to obtain several funding benefits—the ability to raise capital where the separate companies could not raise any; the ability to raise it at a lower cost; the ability to allocate the capital better; and the ability to take on larger projects.

A smaller company which is seeking to grow usually

must raise additional capital. A constant complaint of such smaller growth companies is that raising this capital is a difficult task at the best of times, and a nearly impossible one during bad times. This difficulty is a constraint on growth. Combining with other smaller companies into a larger company may well alleviate this problem and ease the raising of capital. A larger company has more sources of finance available, is a more viable, and thus a less risky company. This benefit is greatest if, by merging, the companies reach a threshold size which permits a public offering.

The second form of the funding benefit is that not only can the combined company actually raise the capital, but it can do so less expensively. Debt and equity cost the bigger combined company less than they do the individual component companies.

Canada's Royal Commission on Corporate Concentration examined this question. It examined 10 empirical studies which used an indirect measure of the capital cost of industries in the United States, United Kingdom, and Canada.[6] Of the studies, three showed that large companies could borrow at a lower rate, five showed no difference, and two showed the opposite. Nevertheless, the Commission concluded that large firms do obtain lower interest rates on bank borrowings, and it speculated that the saving was in the order of one or two percentage points. If two similar sized companies, each with an average capital structure of 40 percent debt and 60 percent equity, merged and could thereby immediately renegotiate and decrease the cost of all of the debt by a full 2 percent, then the increase in market value that would result would be in the order of 3 percent.[7] This is not a significant improvement, and for most mergers, it would be much less. For a combination of two large public companies, it would be negligible.

By combining two companies, the equity market could find that the resulting shares are more attractive because a more robust market has been created and the securities are more marketable. More attractive shares mean less expensive equity. Studies indicate that shares with restricted trading rights sell at an average 35 percent discount below comparable shares which are freely negotiable.[8] This is the extreme situation. The normal merger would result in only a small improvement in share negotiability.

The argument is sometimes made that larger companies and their business managers can add value by their ability to select more desirable investments, that a special form of managerial benefit exists. In a merger between Far-Mar-Co and Farmland Industries, two agricultural cooperatives, Far-Mar-Co felt that a major value-added from the merger would be Farmland's ability to finance a new process that Far-Mar-Co had developed for splitting a wheat kernel into its four basic components without damaging them. Presumably Far-Mar-Co had tried to raise the capital but was unable. If Farmland did indeed ultimately finance the project, did it create value? Only if it could do a better job in picking a good investment than could the capital markets, and if the share market accepts and gives value to this superiority. A company can outperform the capital markets in picking desirable investments, and the markets may give credit for this ability. But to anticipate this with any degree of certainty requires that the company have some unique and obvious insight into the project requiring financing. It may very well be that Farmland did create value because it is in the agricultural business, and it may have been better able to assess the potential of the wheat splitting process than could the agricultural segment of the capital markets. But if a company has no unique insight into a particular business, then it is surely fooling itself if it thinks that it can better allocate capital and choose winning projects than could the capital markets, and that the share market will accept and give value to this. The author's experience as Director of Capital Funding and Evaluation of a large multinational corporation would suggest that, even in a situation where there is some interrelationship between the component companies, allocating capital between competing projects is difficult. Canada's Royal Commission on Corporate Concentration studied whether large diversified firms allocate their capital more efficiently than small firms, and could detect no evidence of such an ability.[9] Nevertheless, this benefit is one that can exist between closely related companies. It surely does not exist elsewhere.

Combining two companies could enable the combined company to take on a large capital-intense project. Some consider this a benefit. Alternative approaches would be to form a joint venture, or to form a stand-alone project that could attract independent project financing. There are mechanisms for companies to take on big projects without the necessity of a merger. Whether or not value is created depends on whether the merger alternative is superior to the other approaches. In some circumstances it might well be, but one of the other mechanisms could be as good, if not superior, in many cases.

Overall, the funding benefit is not a significant one, except where a merger permits a company to go public. In other situations it is of marginal value.

2. Taxes. Different countries have laws which enable two companies which have merged to reduce the taxes paid. These laws vary from country to country and we can only touch on some of them.

A tax benefit that is widely permitted is the write-off of accumulated net operating losses against future earnings. A company with such losses can purchase a profitable company and shelter those profits from taxes until the loss is used up. The acquired company's profits are tax free. This can be a very significant benefit. Some corporate shells have no value other than such accumulated losses. A bankrupt reorganized railroad sought to acquire a profitable division of a large health-care corporation. The division was estimated to be worth $28 million to the health-care company, but worth $50 million to the railroad because of its accumulated losses that would permit it to shelter the division's earnings. This benefit can be very significant.

There is a tax benefit embodied in what was popular advice in the mid 1970s, namely that a company should seek to balance its portfolio of businesses in order to match its cash generators with its cash users. According to this advice a company which is in a mature business, presumably a cash generator, should seek to acquire new and emerging businesses which are cash users. Doing this eliminates the need to return to cash to the shareholders by paying dividends on which the shareholders pay taxes. In countries which do not permit a company to purchase its own stock, such as Australia, it may well be in the interests of the shareholders for the company to invest in other businesses for them and thereby avoid this tax on dividends. But a company almost invariably will be required to pay a price premium when making such an acquisition. Individual shareholders would not. And so it becomes a matter of comparing the tax saving with the premium to determine if a company should do this. In countries which permit a company to purchase its own stock, such as the United States and Canada, the company can thereby return its cash indirectly to the shareholders so that no immediate tax liability is created, but rather only a capital gain at some later time. The shareholders are then able to make their own investments in other companies without suffering a premium. Thus there is no tax benefit in the United States, Canada, and countries which permit the purchase of treasury stock.

Interest payments are tax deductible, which makes debt relatively cheap when compared to equity capital. This means that a company can increase its market value by carrying more debt rather than less. But only up to a point. At high levels of debt, the greater variability of earnings and the concern for bankruptcy lower the market value. However, it is possible to purchase a company with an overly conservative capital structure, increase the debt and thereby increase the value of the firm. A common acquisition strategy is the "leveraged buyout" in which the purchaser puts up a fraction of the purchase price and then borrows the remainder on the assets of the firm being acquired. The sort of company sought for such a leveraged buyout is typically one which has a long history of steady earnings (and hence can support a large amount of debt) but which does not have much debt (it has an overly conservative capital structure). This can be a significant benefit and can result in an increase in market value by as much as 30 percent.

In the United States an acquisition can be structured so that the value of the acquired assets can be raised for the purpose of figuring the depreciation or depletion expense. Doing this lowers the reported income but also lowers the taxes paid. In a sophisticated capital market the net effect would be to increase the market value because of the lower taxes paid, despite the fact that lower earnings are being reported. Empirical evidence of the United States' capital markets indicates that this is indeed the case, but this may be counterproductive in other capital markets dominated by less sophisticated investors who look no further than the reported earnings.[10]

In many western countries, a company can opt for one of several ways of determing its profits by determining which accounting convention it will follow in valuing inventories. One company can buy another, change the accounting convention and raise the inventory values, and thus report lower earnings but pay less tax. It will thereby increase the market value of the company, assuming that inflation will continue at a high level. It should be noted however that it was not necessary for a merger to take place to do this. The incumbent management could have opted to change its accounting conventions itself. This tax benefit could actually be considered a special form of "managerial" benefit in which more competent financial management replaces the less competent.

Tax benefits can be substantial in a merger.

3. Risk. Large companies have a greater ability to bear risk than small companies. They are more able to take on high-risk projects, such as starting into an attractive new industry or plunging into high technology which requires a considerable investment in research and development or taking on a long-lead project in which market conditions can completely change before the project comes to fruition.

Whether value is created depends on the ability of the corporate management to select good investment opportunities. In the start-up situation, for example, the company would in effect be becoming a venture capitalist. Venture capitalism is an industry in and unto itself, requiring unique skills and insight for success.

In terms of innovation, the empirical evidence suggests that larger companies have not been at the cutting edge of major new technologies.[11] The large company's enhanced ability to bear risk seems to be more than overcome by its bureaucratic lethargy, its desire to protect its vested interests, or its inability to attract and hold innovative people.

As for high-risk, long-lead projects, smaller companies can and do combine to do these using mechanisms such as the joint venture. Thus, while value may be created by an enabling merger, value could be created by these other means.

The second form of risk-bearing concerns the desire of many companies to diversify so that their shareholders own part of a diversified portfolio of businesses.

Companies which are ideal purchase candidates for

such diversifications, either because they are countercyclical or because they are in an attractive new industry, are already highly valued by the capital markets. A publicly owned corporation which seeks to diversify into other businesses is doing nothing for the shareholders that they could not do for themselves. However the company will almost invariably pay a price premium over and over the market value, shareholders do not, and so the company is actually doing harm to its shareholders. This is the sort of help that no shareholder needs! However, in an economy where the majority of shareholders are not sophisticated and are not diversified, it might well be in the interests of these shareholders for the company to act paternally and to diversify for them, even if it does have to pay a price premium over and above the market value to do it.

In the case of a closely held company, a common situation is for the shareholders to have a significant portion of their wealth locked into the one company with no easy way to take the money out to diversify their own portfolios. In this circumstance also it could well be in the interests of the shareholders for the company to diversify for them, even though it may have to pay a price premium.

4. Familial. A merger may give a familial benefit by providing entree to the ruling family who controls an economy, by providing some minority representation required by law, or by satisfying some nationalistic demands thus opening a foreign economy to business.

In some third-world countries a key factor in considering a relationship is not what a local partner can bring in the way of operational benefits, but what the partner can bring in terms of contacts and friends in high places.

Many countries have nationalistic local equity requirements. Mining projects in Australia must have 50 percent local equity, and a foreign company may seek a local partner who may bring nothing more than "Australianism," a familial benefit.

Costs

The value-added that results from a merger of two firms is the net of the benefits less the costs. Merging two companies is a costly business, and it is necessary to consider these costs.

1. Front-end costs. Front-end costs are for searching, negotiating, auditing, registering, and closing a deal. They are paid to the company staff, attorneys, accountants, consultants, bankers. Depending on the size of the acquisition, they usually vary in the range from .5 percent for the largest purchase up to 10 percent for a very small one.

2. Direct ongoing costs. Direct ongoing costs include the increased pay and benefit packages that are so frequently paid to the acquired company's employees. Smaller companies can pay with hope; bigger companies cannot, and they need internal uniformity. These costs also include increased government regulation. Bigger companies seem to attract more scrutiny than do smaller companies, and this is expensive. It also includes the cost of increased overheads. A verse by Gail Cooke in *The Wall Street Journal* says much:

> *Ready Cash*
> My money problems would vanish
> If I'd just keep the oath I swore:
> To live as cheaply after pay-day
> As I did the day before.

Many a lean company has turned to blubber under the auspices of a well-heeled parent.

These first two costs are easy to identify and quantify, and companies sometimes do it. However the remaining four costs are difficult to quantify and are often forgotten until after an acquisition has been completed.

3. Managerial. These are the costs of losing key and experienced people as a result of the acquisition. A study done by the Chicago-based consulting firm of Hayes/Hill, Inc. of 200 chief executives of acquired firms, all of whom intended to stay after the merger, found that 86 executives, or 43 percent, had left within two years.[12] This is an expensive loss, especially if the acquired company is in a game of Bridge, to use the earlier analogy. The biggest headache after an acquisition is often the personnel problems with management.

This cost also includes the cost of imposing managerial systems on the acquired company. In a study done of entrepreneurial firms acquired by a larger company, it was found that 40 percent of the entrepreneur's time subsequent to acquisition was spent filling out corporate reports and responding to corporate demands, an activity that many consider to be of marginal benefit to the business.

Finally, there is the cost of demotivation. An entrepreneur works long hours each day to make his company go. Having sold out at a high price, it is difficult for the now wealthy entrepreneur to remain as motivated. He has made it, now spend time with the family.

4. Learning costs. Learning costs are the costs of mistakes, as the new management team learns from experience about the new business. Colgate-Palmolive, a manufacturer of soaps, detergents, and toiletries, acquired Helena Rubinstein, a cosmetics firm. The cosmetic business proved to be very different from Colgate's, and Colgate made serious mistakes. Several years later Colgate sold Helena Rubinstein for a fraction of the original $142 million acquisition price.

A story of an Australian station owner comes to mind. When this gentleman was 18, both of his parents were killed in an unfortunate light airplane accident, and he inherited a large sheep station. He decided to do a grand tour of Europe, even though he had never visited the major cities of Australia. He was in Germany and climbed into a Mercedes taxi, the first Mercedes he had ever seen. He asked the driver what the hood emblem was. Somewhat surprised, the German driver indicated that it was his machine-gun site. A look of disbelief from the Australian prompted the driver to correct his story—it was actually a torpedo site, the whole cab was a torpedo used to run down unwary pedestrians. Still the Australian was not convinced, and so the taxi driver proceeded to demonstrate. Pointing to a little old lady some 200 meters ahead, the taxi driver took off and aimed straight for her. At the last minute he swerved, narrowly missing the lady. There was a thump, a scream, pedestrians waved wildly—white faced, the driver spun around to see what had happened. Whereupon the Australian said, "Blimey, mate, you would have missed her, if I hadn't opened my door." The point of the story is that you should not assume that new passengers comprehend the games that are played within your organization. And corporations do indeed play games. One commonly played is "Cut the Capital Budget." In its extreme form, a division comes in and asks for three times as much capital as it needs, and the corporate management aggressively cuts the budget to one third of the request. Everyone is happy. The corporate management has saved money, and the division management has what it needs. A big New York firm gutted five out of its six major acquisitions before it realized that it was playing this game, but that its new presidents were not.

5. Opportunity costs. While the corporate management is learning, sometimes desperately, about its new business, it can easily forget its own traditional business and incur opportunity costs. While Colgate-Palmolive was trying to figure out what to do with Helena Rubinstein, the top management had to pay less attention to its own basic business, making it more likely that its major competitor, Procter & Gamble, would make further inroads into its traditional soap, detergent, and toiletry businesses.

R.J. Reynolds, the major tobacco company, diversified aggressively by acquiring other major companies such as Sea-Land (transport) and Del Monte (food). Presumably it did this because it feared for the future of the tobacco industry. While pursuing this strategy, R.J. Reynolds lost market share in its traditional market to its major competitor, Philip Morris, and it was not successful in introducing low-tar tobacco nor substitutes for tobacco cigarettes. These were significant opportunity costs to R.J. Reynolds.

6. Multibusiness discount. The final cost is nonoperational in nature. The more complicated and multifaceted a business becomes, the more difficult it is for the capital markets to value it accurately. Thus, there is a tendency for two dissimilar businesses to be valued at a lower amount when they are combined than when they are separate. This effect seems to be so pervasive that it should be considered a potential cost in any combination of dissimilar businesses.

We now have a framework which permits a careful look at the various strategies and decision points in buying and selling companies.

Section Two
Acquiring Companies

The decision rule to guide a director in determining whether the company should buy another is:

BUY IF THE VALUE-ADDED EXCEEDS THE PRICE PREMIUM.

The value-added is the increase in market value that would result from merging the two companies. The price premium is the excess to be paid above the stand-alone value of the selling company.

The value-added less the price premium is a measure of how much better off the buying shareholders would be if the purchase is consummated. They are better off only if the value-added realized exceeds the price premium paid, hence the decision rule. If the market value of the company to be bought is $30 million, and the purchase price is $40 million cash, then the price premium is $10 million. If the value-added is $15 million, then the increase in wealth of the buying shareholders is the $15 million value-added less the $10 million premium, $5 million. If $50 million cash is paid, then the drop in value of the buying company, the loss to the buying shareholders, will be $5 million.

The Buy Decision Point

When a director is faced with a decision of whether or not to concur with the purchase of another company, his task is to determine the proposed premium, and then compare this with the expected value-added. The initial step (Step 1) is to ascertain what indeed is the purchase price. If cash is paid, then the purchase price is apparent. If stock of the acquiring company is to be offered, then the purchase price may not be the present market value of the offered shares.

The current market value of the acquiring company's shares may not reflect all of the information about the company; some important things may not have been announced. If it does not reflect favorable information, then the shares are undervalued and the actual purchase price is higher than the current market value of the securities to be offered. If the shares do not reflect negative information, then they are overvalued and the actual purchase price is less. When stock is to be offered, its value should be scrutinized carefully.

The next step (Step 2) is to estimate the target company's stand-alone value. This becomes a matter of evaluating whether the current market price of the target company accurately reflects its real stand-alone value. It could be that the market price does not reflect unannounced negative information and should be adjusted downward accordingly. A director should be most interested in the thoroughness of any "due diligence" meeting with the selling management. Such a meeting should focus on unknown negative aspects. The market price of a selling company frequently moves up in anticipation of an acquisition. Thus the current market price of a widely recognized takeover target may not reflect the underlying economics of the company, but rather, the expected purchase price. A study of 15 major takeovers in the United States in 1978 and 1979 showed that the target companies' price per share rose 28 percent on average in the month prior to the takeover announcement.[13] Such overstatements of real value need to be eliminated.

It is possible that the market has underestimated the selling company's prospects and undervalues it, making it a bargain. Thus it can be argued that the company is actually worth more than its current market value, and the premium is less than at first appears. A frequent rationale given by a chief executive officer (CEO) for an acquisition is that the target company represents an attractive new industry, and that the acquiring company should be in it. This amounts to a claim that the market is underestimating the target company's prospects; hence, the company is undervalued, and the proposed premium is less than it appears. A director would need to assess just what gives the CEO such superior insight into the prospects and value of the company, and why the current market price is incorrect. Such superior insight is possible in the case of a small target company in an unknown industry, traded on a lesser exchange. Such superiority is less likely for a large, well-known company traded on a major exchange.

Even if a director accepts that the market is underestimating a target company, the buying company can only benefit its shareholders if, as a result of the acquisition and within a short time thereafter, the market will reassess the value of the acquired company and make an appropriate adjustment to the value of the surviving corporation. If the market never accepts the error in its past valuation of the target company, the buying company's shareholders will never receive the benefits of the CEO's superior insight.

Thus the premium, the corrected purchase price less the corrected stand-alone value, is computed (Step 3). In the United States, the average premium paid for publicly held companies in the late 1970s, assuming that the market prices one month prior to announcement of the acquisition were a reasonable estimate of the real value, was in the order of 60 percent.[14] With private, closely held companies it was probably less. In Australia, average premiums appear to be in the order of 40 percent for publicly traded companies. In Canada, premiums averaged 27.3 percent over the period 1960-75.[15] In Hong Kong, where it is possible to do a creeping take-over, the premium can be virtually zero. In any particular situation the premium paid can be anything; the demand of some selling shareholders and the willingness to pay of some acquiring companies appear to be open-ended.

The next step (Step 4) is to assess the value-added. Determining the value-added is a matter of focusing on each possible benefit and considering if it would be significant in the particular situation, and then focusing on each cost and considering its significance. It is easy to point to many benefits; it is quite another matter to realize them. A prudent director would insist on a detailed enumeration of the postmerger action plans (which actual plants are to be closed and so forth) before accepting that there are any benefits at all. The very word *synergism* has fallen into disrepute because synergistic benefits have been cited so often to justify an acquisition, but have so frequently not materialized. Hence the use here of the term *value-added*.

The final step (Step 5) is to compare the premium with the value-added. If the premium is greater, a nay vote is indicated; if the value-added is greater, a yea vote is indicated. Once a director of a buying company has determined that the expected value-added exceeds the anticipated premium, then he can be assured that such an acquisition should add to the market value of the buying company and to the wealth of its shareholders.

From an investor's viewpoint, following the above steps will assist in judging whether a company's share value will rise or fall and whether to buy or to sell.

Section IV provides an actual example (Du Pont's purchase of Conoco) of the above procedure for a director and the procedure for an investor.

Buy Strategy 1—The Pursuit of Value-Added

But where should a company look to find such attractive purchases which add to the company's shareholders' wealth? This is a bigger question than merely making a buy decision in a particular circumstance. Committing a corporation to a desirable strategy will result in many attractive acquisition proposals. Deciding on what general strategy to which to commit a corporation becomes one of determining where the value-added is likely to be the greatest, where the benefits will be largest and the costs least; or one of determining where the company is most likely to find bargains. The pursuit of value-added will be considered first.

Horizontal Acquisitions

Consider first a horizontal acquisition in which a company buys a similar company, its competitor or complement. Assume, for the purpose of illustration, that Ford Motor seeks to buy a competitor which is strong in small cars. We can determine whether this is desirable by considering each of the benefits and costs that could result. The benefits are:

Sales and marketing. Such a merger could lead to a rationalization of the product line, the elimination of overlapping models, and could provide Ford more offerings in the small, front-wheel drive end of the car market.

Costs and production. By combining the firms, overheads could be eliminated, staff rationalized, and greater quantities of materials purchased, thus permitting quantity discounts and design expenses to be written off over longer product runs.

Research and technology. Any research that Ford has done in low pollution engine design would be applicable to the acquired competitor's product line, and vice versa.

Resource. Greater specialization could be affected at the various plants, eliminating the need for the companies to manufacture different models in the same plant. As well, by giving Ford a larger presence in the small car market, a business which seems to do better in hard times, there is some possibility of converting some Ford plants to the production of less expensive, small cars during recessionary times, thus keeping them utilized.

Managerial. With judicious culling, the quality of management could be raised. The better management techniques and systems, already adapted to the car industry, could survive.

The nonoperational benefits (funding, taxes, risk, and familial benefits) will not be considered here in determining a strategy because these can be found anywhere. They do not give guidance as to what direction a company should take or what general strategy it should pursue. Nevertheless, they would be considered in a particular instance or decision point. The costs are:

Front-end, direct and managerial. There is nothing unique about horizontal mergers that would make these costs any more or less than for any other type of merger. Ford would expect to pay similar costs for this merger as with any other.

Learning. Because the surviving executives know the car business, there would be small learning costs.

Opportunity. The executives will not turn their attention away from Ford's traditional business while they dabble in the new one because it is the same business. Thus it is not likely that the company will suffer opportunity costs.

Multibusiness discount. And because the resulting company will not become multifaceted and more difficult to value, because the same security analysts will be involved, the combined company should not suffer a drop in value in response to such market uncertainty.

Looking back at the benefits and costs, it can be seen that the opportunity for significant benefits is large, and the likelihood of significant costs is small. Thus the value-added could be significant. This is the usual situation with horizontal acquisitions. A first strategy for any corporation is the horizontal one, the purchase of complements and competitors.

The example given, a merger between Ford and a competitor, is one that probably could not be effected in practice because the United States has antitrust laws which would prohibit such a merger between two companies in such a concentrated industry. The intended purpose of these laws is to prevent excessive concentration which would permit excessive profits. The possibility of pleading distress, or of a change in attitude under a new administration, may change this. Public policy will be discussed more fully in the Postscript. But there are many opportunities, even in the United States, to conduct a horizontal strategy. This is especially true of smaller companies and on a product-line basis.

There have been many successes by companies that have followed this strategy. Waste Management and Browning-Ferris each achieved spectacular and successful growth by acquiring many small refuse companies. U.S. Life has grown by acquiring and integrating many small life companies. These are several of the more recent and better known success stories. Many small companies in the early phases of their growth are following this strategy successfully. Many of today's giants followed this strategy in their early years. General Motors, for example, grew in its initial phase by merging many small manufacturers. The list is long.

Conglomerate Acquisitions

We now go to the other extreme and consider a conglomerate merger in which a company buys a complete stranger, one that has no relationship to its existing business.

The rationales usually cited for such a merger are to permit entry into an attractive business, or to permit diversification. For the purpose of illustration, assume that Ford seeks to buy a health care company which continues to experience rapid growth, or Ford seeks to buy a foreign gold company whose earnings are counter cyclical to its own.

The immediate problem with this strategy is that the

market also recognizes the attractiveness of the health care and gold companies, and these already command high prices. For Ford to come in and pay this high price, and then the additional premium, might not be doing a favor for Ford's shareholders. Ford's shareholders also find these companies attractive and can buy (and probably have bought) the stock on their own account; hence the high price that these stocks already command. But the shareholders do not need to pay the additional price premium that Ford would. To justify the premium that it must pay, Ford has to contribute something extra that the shareholders cannot, the value-added, that results from integrating the companies. The possible benefits are:

Sales and marketing. There is nothing that Ford could contribute to either the health care or gold company to help in marketing its products, or vice versa.

Costs and production. There is virtually no rationalization of overheads possible, no improved purchasing, and no longer production runs because the product lines are so dissimilar.

Research and technology. It is of no help to Ford that the health care company has a team of brilliant scientists developing new intravenous solutions. Nor is Ford's engine technology of any use to the gold miners.

Resource. It is not possible to produce automobiles through an intravenous bottling plant, or a gold mine.

Managerial. It is unlikely that the Ford executives even know the key players in the health care or the gold mining industries, and these are sophisticated games of Bridge. Ford would have little chance of competing successfully.

Because of the dissimilar nature of the businesses in a conglomerate deal, there is little chance of operational benefits, benefits which come from integrating the operations. The costs are:

Front-end, direct and managerial. There is nothing unique about conglomerate mergers that would produce higher costs in these areas; these would be expected to be average.

Learning. If Ford acquired the health care or the gold mining company and then insisted on running these companies, it should expect to incur significant learning costs. What works in the automobile industry does not necessarily work elsewhere, and Ford should expect to take several years to appreciate the subtleties of these other industries. Such on-the-job training for top management can be very expensive.

Opportunity. And while the Ford management is learning its new business, and possibly trying to rectify mistakes already made, they are likely to spend less time on their traditional business, to its detriment.

Multibusiness discount. As a result of conglomerating, Ford would become more complex and its prospects more difficult to assess. Thus Ford should expect a downward effect on its market price as a result of this market uncertainty.

Looking at the benefits and the costs in a conglomerate merger shows that the value-added is unlikely to be significant. It could even be negative, a value-lost. Of course, in any particular case it is possible to have some worthwhile nonoperational benefits that would save the day. To summarize, the nonoperational benefits that could be of significant value are: the company could reach a threshold size that would permit it to go public; or it could better utilize the assets' debt-carrying capacity; or it could reduce taxes by utilizing accumulated losses or by increasing depreciation or depletion expenses; or it could receive a familial benefit. The other nonoperational benefits are usually insignificant or nonexistent.

Vertical Acquisitions

A vertical acquisition is one in which the company buys one of its customers or suppliers. For example, Ford purchases a chain of its independent dealerships or buys a component manufacturer.

This strategy, in terms of value-added, is between the horizontal and conglomerate strategies. There is obvious potential for at least some value-added, although not much in the typical situation. However, one major justification for a vertical acquisition is as a defensive strategy, to stop a supplier from going direct or to stop a customer from developing its own supply capabilities. This strategy is justified, not so much in terms of value-added, but in terms of protecting existing value. This can be a worthwhile strategy for the company's shareholders.

Value-Added and Relatedness

We can demonstrate the basic concept graphically by plotting the benefits, costs, and hence the value-added against the relatedness of the two companies that merge. (See Exhibit 2.)

Looking at Exhibit 2, the operational benefits are greatest when there is a high degree of relatedness between the companies—a horizontal merger—and are least when there is a low degree of relatedness between the companies—a conglomerate merger. The benefit curve bells upward because of the existence of resource benefits that can increase as the relatedness decreases, a significant one of which is the utilization of resources during recessionary periods as in the example of the manufacturer of cheap mobile homes and luxury recreational vehicles.

Looking at Exhibit 2, the costs are lowest when there is a high degree of relatedness—the horizontal merger—and are greatest due to increasing learning, opportunity, and multibusiness discount costs when there is a low degree of relatedness—the conglomerate merger.

The value-added is the difference between the benefits and the costs. Where the benefits exceed the costs we have positive value-added; where they are less we have negative value-added, or value-lost. This graph says essentially the same thing as the *Economist* in an article titled "Return of the Octopus":

> Takeovers to diversify are back in fashion. . . . Companies now shy away from the word "conglomerate." The buzzword is "diversification" . . . more sin than synergy?
> . . . big conglomerates are often inefficient. They may douse entrepreneurial ability under an avalanche of monthly reports. They may substitute management that knows nothing sophisticatedly for one with intuition based on experience and judgment. They may lead to a loss of accountability as companies sink out of sight.[16]

Exhibit 2

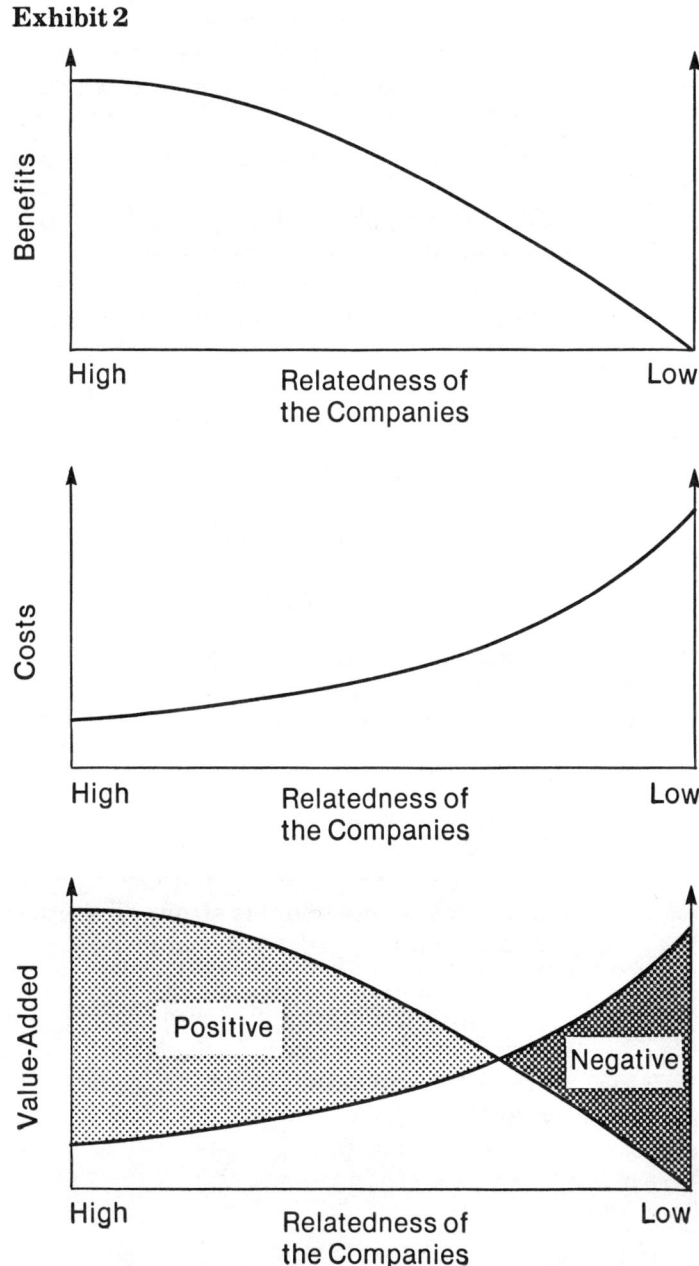

What the *Economist* refers to as *synergy* we are calling *benefits*, and what the *Economist* refers to as *sin* we are calling *costs*. The *Economist* was questioning the existence of the Exhibit 2 fish tail, the negative value-added.

The graphs shown in Exhibit 2 are for a publicly owned company. For a closely held private company in which the shareholders are not free to diversify themselves, there can be a clear benefit from diversity, and thus the tail of the fish, the negative value-added, is smaller or even nonexistent. Even in this situation though, the shareholders are usually better off if the company seeks fairly related acquisitions, thus permitting some beneficial interactions and avoiding the large costs that can come with extreme diversity.

Strengths and Weaknesses

We know that a company should seek first to acquire its complements and competitors (the horizontal deal), then its customers and suppliers (the vertical deal), and should perhaps forget about strangers (the conglomerate deal). Where to look in developing an acquisition strategy has been considerably narrowed. But we can do better. The next step is to match strengths and weaknesses, to buy companies that are strong where yours is weak, weak where yours is strong. The effect of doing this is to magnify greatly the value-added.

Matching strengths and weaknesses is a creative process. One technique is to analyze the company and its possible acquisition using the framework for operational benefits:

Sales and marketing.
  Where are we strong? Who is weak in this area?
  Where are we weak? Who is strong in this area?

Costs and production . . . .

Research and technology . . . .

Resource . . . .

Managerial . . . .

Thus a director could influence his company to develop an acquisition strategy which would be a statement of desired compatibilities. Such a statement would direct the company in its search and save considerable argument later.

A security analyst can ascertain a company's strategy from interviews with the management, public statements as to strategy, and from an evaluation of the company's past actions. This will give valuable insight as to whether the company is going to create wealth or not, and to what degree its shareholders will participate in that wealth.

Joint Ventures

The conceptual framework developed for considering mergers and acquisitions can also be applied to joint ventures. International joint ventures in developing countries could well be the hallmark of the 1980s as they are able to handle emerging nationalistic aspirations. A common arrangement is for the local partner to provide local ownership (familial benefit), while the multinational partners provide marketing, operational, research, technological, and perhaps funding benefits. Only contributing parties are typically invited to participate; hence joint ventures are inherently horizontal in nature. Thus the entire venture can be considered a creation of value, value-added.

A horizontal merger and a joint venture between two companies can be illustrated diagramatically as in Exhibit 3.

Buy Strategy 2—The Pursuit of Bargains

In considering companies to buy we have been looking for situations which give value-added, favorable interactions between the two companies. However, it is possible for the buying company to win for its shareholders, not with value-added, but by obtaining a bargain, a company which is undervalued and for which a negative premium is paid.

Even with publicly traded companies on sophisticated Class I capital markets, it is reasonable to assume that at any moment history will reveal that some 50 percent of companies were overvalued and some 50 percent of companies were undervalued, relative to the market as a whole. One strategy would be simply to buy the undervalued companies, the bargains. However if the buying company does not have some superior insight, it would have only an even chance of buying such an undervalued company. But it always pays a price in excess of the market value, and so the odds of winning when this premium is taken into account are considerably less than even.

Perhaps the company does possess superior insight in that, by using sophisticated techniques such as discounted cash flow, it can judge the true value of a company better than the markets can. And because of the

Exhibit 3

Merger

Joint Venture

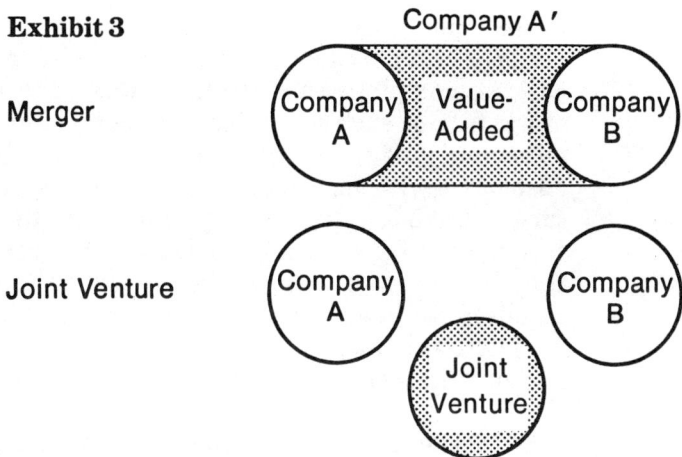

buying company's formidable reputation, if it does pay a price in excess of the market value, the capital market will defer to the company's judgment and revalue the acquired company upward. Such a revaluation would be necessary for the buying shareholders to win too.

People with knowledge of discounted cash flow techniques will recognize the difficulty in making a satisfactory cash flow projection, especially if the company does not know the business being bought, and of then selecting an appropriate rate to discount the cash flow projection to present values. Many doubt that it is possible to select such undervalued companies in a sophisticated capital market. On the other hand, with an unsophisticated capital market, there may well be opportunities for a company so to find bargains.

The stock markets seem to undervalue certain classes of companies consistently. Two groups that could be considered to represent bargains are the multibusinesses and conglomerates. Recently formed conglomerates and old-line multibusinesses such as General Electric complain that they are undervalued by the markets. But such an undervaluation is due to a very reasonable judgment by the markets of the high costs associated with such diversity. Perhaps the only way to turn this to advantage is to buy such a multibusiness or conglomerate and then break it up into its components, thereby eliminating the costs and low valuation. This has been the basis of some takeover attempts in which an alternate slate of directors proposed this strategy and offered themselves for election.

A market is made up of people buying and selling shares for profit. People are emotional and the market is also. The basic driving forces are fear and greed. When a company or industry comes under strong pressure, the market reacts. There is some evidence it overreacts. Thus a company's or industry's shares may fall too far, giving a bargain hunter the opportunity to buy in at a low price and benefit from the subsequent market adjustment. This can be described as a contrary strategy: Do the opposite to the market; buy when it is selling and begs you to buy, sell when it is buying and begs you to sell. Some individuals seem to succeed at this strategy, but most probably do not—not when account is taken of the costs of trading. A company would have even less chance of winning with this strategy; it faces an enormous premium over and above the trading costs.

Some experts suggest that the whole stock market may be undervalued, due to all-pervasive inflation.[17] This view holds that the market recognizes the negative aspect of inflation, namely that inflation causes bogus inflationary profits which are taxed heavily; but it does not appreciate the positive aspect, namely that liabilities are paid off with cheap dollars. While this is interesting, it is difficult to see how to capitalize on a situation where the whole world is a bargain.

The best opportunity for obtaining bargains is to buy closely held companies. There is no market to guide the sellers, and by skillful negotiating, the buying company may convince the selling company to sell at a bargain price—it may obtain a "negotiation bargain." Sellers of closely held companies would always be wise to have skillful negotiators represent them in an acquisition situation. Beatrice Foods, a U.S. conglomerate, has a reputation for being a tough negotiator and for buying closely held companies at bargain prices. If Beatrice has done well by its shareholders, it is because of this factor and not because of any value-added. For the most part its purchases have been too dissimilar to permit significant value-added.

Closely held companies could well sell out at bargain prices for a number of very good reasons:

Diversifiers. A common situation is for a successful businessman to have a large portion of his own wealth tied up in his closely held company, to have no ready means of effectively diversifying his own personal wealth as his shares are not easily marketed, or because the sale of some of his shares to another person would be odious. It may well be worthwhile to such a person to sell out at a bargain price so that his whole wealth is not dependent on the continued success of the one company.

Cash needy. Closely held companies can sometimes be bought at a bargain price because of extreme cash needs, such as the need to pay estate taxes where the majority shareholder has recently died. Another reason along these lines is that closely held companies frequently sell because of a frustrating inability to finance growth. This has been discussed under funding benefits in the previous section.

Time pressured. Time pressures sometimes result in bargain-priced companies. These pressures can be caused by a court-ordered divestiture, as when ITT was ordered to divest Avis within a certain period of time. In this case ITT managed to relieve the pressure by obtaining an extension on the time limit. Another extreme time pressure situation is the distress sale. Rather than go into bankruptcy, a company is sold quickly at a bargain price. The large investment banking company of Shearson Loeb Rhoades, Inc. was built by buying other companies, in distress, at bargain prices. Shearson's strategy was actually double-barreled. Shearson sought bargains which were also compatible and that would yield value-added.

Problem child. Many large multibusinesses have divisions which do not seem to fit well with the other businesses and which do not perform to expectation. This represents a problem for the management. If new management is in charge that does not need to justify past actions, it may be only too willing to unload such divisions, and at bargain prices. New management at G. D. Searle embarked on just such a major selling program upon taking control. This may be the major source of bargains in future years as multibusinesses and conglomerates are dismantled.

A popular reason given for acquiring companies is

that the current market value is less than the book value. If the intent of the acquiring company is to do an asset strip, to sell off and redeploy assets in a way that society values more highly, then the argument may be valid. A market value less than book value may well indicate such a bargain. If, however, the acquiring company intends to continue business as usual and cites the further justification that it is cheaper to buy than to build, then it begs the question. What the company should do is neither buy nor build; it should do nothing. Buying such a company and then continuing to operate it as before is not a bargain. If the capital markets are given no reason to revalue the acquired company upwards, then the buying shareholders profit naught.

Diversifying Successfully

However, there does seem to be a compelling need that some companies feel to diversify. The challenge is to do this without falling into the conglomeration trap in which the premium exceeds the value-added. Listed are a number of techniques.

International ventures. Joint ventures in foreign countries provide significant opportunities for diversification for two reasons. First, they are often tied to foreign markets which provide some measure of protection against the vagaries of the home market; and second, they are typically structured so a company's commitment is relatively small, enabling it to participate in other ventures and gain protection from greater numbers.

Resource commonalities. The company could do

a horizontal acquisition in which the value-added is a "resource" benefit. In this case a different market is served, but the same resources are used. The example cited earlier was Fleetwood Enterprises, a manufacturer of luxury recreational vehicles and cheap mobile homes, products which are very different and counter-cyclical but which use the same physical and human resources.

Linked chain. The third strategy is to make horizontal acquisitions, but to build on different and acquired skills. Hence the company proliferates into many different businesses, each linked with another, but bearing less and less relationship to the original core business or strength.

Catalyst. A fourth approach is to act as a catalyst. It is not necessary for an acquired company to provide value-added with the acquiring company. It is possible to do this with other acquired businesses. A company would look for a fractured industry which offers potential for rationalizing between companies, and it would act as a catalyst by putting together a larger and more efficient company made up of many small components. An example is Exxon Enterprises, Exxon's office equipment subsidiary, which is made up of small companies that relate to each other but not to the parent.

A variation of this approach is that pursued by some bigger companies in which they seek to add a second and third leg to their operational base. Thus several unrelated diversifying acquisitions are made, but subsequent acquisitions relate to these new businesses. The success of this strategy depends on the magnitude of the value-added achieved with the subsequent acquisitions.

Management expertise. The fifth possibility is to seek an unrelated company where management benefits can be brought to bear. This requires the purchase of a company which is playing in a game of Fish, and where general techniques can be introduced that will give a competitive advantage. The key problem is to recognize the game of Fish. Most games are probably Bridge, and this is difficult to do without actually having firsthand experience in the industry in which the company operates.

Nonoperational benefits. By seeking nonoperational benefits a company may win with an unrelated acquisition. The funding and risk benefits offer little significant benefit. Tax benefits, where an unrelated company that permits utilization of a net operating loss is acquired, can be significant. Or the familial benefit, where the acquired company provides an entree into the acquiring company's traditional business, but in another country, can be significant.

Bargains. The seventh approach is to seek a bargain. This is very difficult when considering publicly held companies, except in unsophisticated markets, and the best chance is to seek a closely held company. This offers the possibility of a negotiation bargain. Or the company may sell at a bargain price for one of the reasons cited earlier: personal diversification, cash or time pressures, or the problem child.

Foothold/Venture capitalist. An eighth technique is the venture capital approach, which is particularly useful for entering an attractive new business. The technique is for the company to support an entrepreneurial effort, usually by lending cash which is convertible to an equity position should the new company succeed. It is usually a hands-off situation where the large company gives nothing more than cash and perhaps some management advice when requested by the entrepreneurial company. Using this approach a company can in effect monitor many emerging industries at little cost in the hope that one or two of them will blossom and provide a foothold for subsequent expansion. Business Development Services, Inc., has been set up by General Electric of the United States to pursue just such a venture capital approach.

If a company does have a compelling need to diversify by buying unrelated companies, and cannot pursue any of the options listed above, at the very least it should seek to act as nothing more than a holding company. It should refrain from integrating the company into its operations. Doing this will make it impossible to obtain any operational benefits from the acquisition, but because the acquired company is unrelated, these are virtually impossible anyway. The key is that the management, learning, and opportunity costs will be minimized and the loss is limited to the price premium paid. When General Electric first acquired Utah International, the management of General Electric was reputedly forbidden to have any contact with the management of Utah, presumably for fear of incurring such costs.

Empirical Evidence

Many studies have been done on the success of acquisition programs. For our purpose we will look only at two more recent studies that distinguish between the type (horizontal, conglomerate, and so forth) of acquisition, and that focus on the total compound annual return to shareholders. The studies which satisfy these requirements were conducted in Canada by the Royal Commission on Corporate Concentration.

Study 1—Multiple Classifications

Richard P. Rumelt, in *Strategy, Structure and Economic Performance*, studied the performance of 200 of the larger firms in the United States at three different points in time.[18] His study did not consider the compound annual return to investors and so will not be reported here. However, the Canadian Royal Commission on Corporate Concentration (RCCC) used Rumelt's classification system of corporate structures and did study the compound annual return to shareholders from dividends and appreciation.[19] The RCCC studied Canada's largest 200 companies over the period 1960 to 1975. The structures studied and their percent of compound annual return were:

Single business................................. 8.9%
   Firms that are basically committed to a single business, and that largely refrained from acquisitions.

Constrained-dominant 19.1%
   Firms that have built on one particular strength, skill, or resource associated with the original activity, but which still obtain a preponderance of their revenues from a single business.

Constrained-related 20.3%
   Firms that have gone further than the constrained-dominant businesses; that have also built on one particular strength, skill,

or resource associated with the original activity. Each business activity is related to almost all of the others, but the firms obtain a lesser proportion of their revenues from the original business than do the constrained-dominant firms.

Linked-dominant 16.3%
These are firms that have built by relating new businesses to some strength or skill already possessed, but not always the same one, thus becoming active in different businesses. But the original business still dominates.

Linked-related 12.2%
Firms that have gone beyond the linked-dominant firms, and have built by relating new businesses to some strength or skill already possessed, but not always the same one, thus becoming active in widely disparate businesses no one of which predominates.

Vertical-dominant 8.3%
Vertically integrated firms that obtain a preponderance of their revenues from a single business.

Unrelated-dominant 10.2%
These are firms that have built without regard to relationships between new businesses and current activities, but that still obtain a preponderance of their revenues from a single business.

Unrelated businesses 8.1%
Firms that have continued beyond the unrelated-dominant firms, and have built without regard to relationships between new and current businesses to the point where no one business predominates.

Using these cross-sectional measurements, and recognizing that corporations following one particular strategy would have built from single to dominant to related (or unrelated) businesses, we can consider four possible strategies and develop a composite picture which gives an indication of the performance characteristics that we could expect as a firm moves along a strategy path.

1. Horizontal strategy (H): firms go from single (8.9 percent), to constrained-dominant (19.1 percent), to constrained-related (20.3 percent).
2. Linked horizontal strategy (H^L): firms go from single (8.9 percent), to linked-dominant (16.3 percent), to linked-related (12.2 percent). This is the linked chain strategy discussed earlier in the section on successful diversification.
3. Vertical strategy (V): firms go from single (8.9 percent), to vertical-dominant (8.3 percent).
4. Conglomerate strategy (C): firms go from single (8.9 percent), to unrelated-dominant (10.2 percent), to unrelated (8.1 percent).

The composite picture is plotted in Exhibit 4.

As we expected, the economic performance in terms of returns to shareholders is best with the pure horizontal strategy which gives excellent results and falls rap-

Exhibit 4

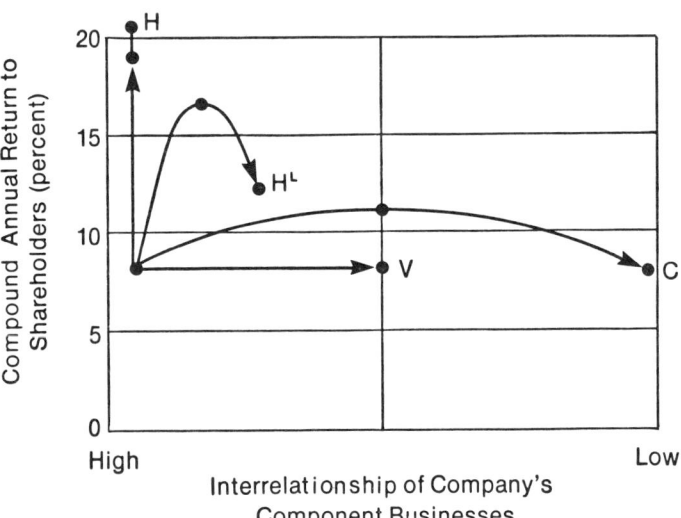

Interrelationship of Company's Component Businesses

idly as strategies which result in fewer interrelationships are pursued. The worst is the conglomerate strategy which is actually detrimental to its shareholders.

An examination of the 200 U.S. companies that were studied by Rumelt indicates that few of them followed the idealized paths shown above and that internal growth also played a part. This is probably true also of the Canadian situation. Thus the return percentages shown should not be regarded as a firm measure of what resulted from the identified acquisition strategies. However, a company following a clearly defined and maintained horizontal, vertical, or conglomerate strategy should expect to pass through the structural forms that were studied and should expect to experience relative results that are at least comparable with those measured.

Study 2—Conglomerates

Mason and Goudzwaard compared the return to stockholders of 22 conglomerates in the United States from 1962 to 1967 with 22 portfolios made up of single companies selected to mirror the component businesses of the conglomerates.[20] Even though conglomerates were still in favor in 1967, the mirror portfolios outperformed them in 19 of the 22 comparisons.

Canada's Royal Commission on Corporate Concentration did a similar comparison in Canada between 10 conglomerates and 10 mirror portfolios over a longer period, from 1960 to 1975.[21] They also found that the portfolios, averaging 12.7 percent per year to the shareholders, outperformed the conglomerates, which averaged 9.4 percent per year, 3.3 percent less.

The Royal Commission went further and examined how much of this 3.3 percent shortfall could be attributed to the payment of a price premium which averaged 27.3 percent. By penalizing the portfolios with this premium, and then repeating the computations, they found that 2.7 percent of the difference was accounted for by the premium. Presumably, the remaining .6 percent was due to poorer operational performance and/or the valuation discount that multibusinesses attract. These results can be shown graphically as in Exhibit 5 on the following page.

Defenders of conglomerates make several points.

Exhibit 5

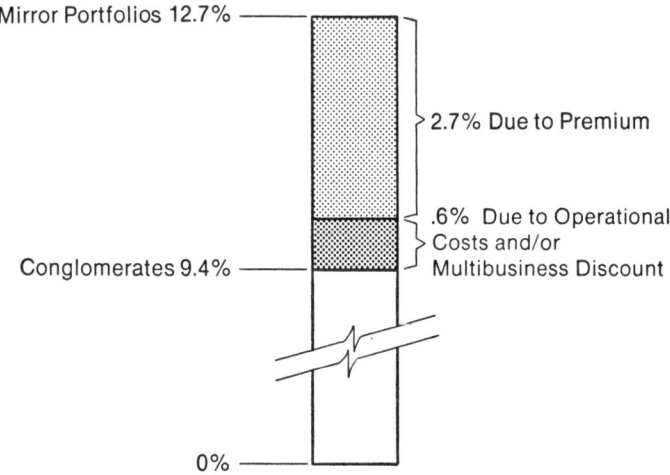

First, that some companies seek to conglomerate because of the need to reduce their dependence on their own suffering industry; that while a conglomerate might do poorly, it would have done even worse if it had chosen not to make such a move. This argument may be valid, at least partially. While the company itself might have done better by conglomerating, its shareholders perhaps did not. The shareholders may have been better off with a return of cash whereupon they could have diversified elsewhere without paying a price premium, and without causing value-lost. Nevertheless, it would be enlightening to do a number of industry-based studies, comparing the returns to shareholders of those that conglomerated, with those that did not.

The second argument is that the jury is still out, that it is too soon to judge conglomerates, that theirs is a long-term strategy which has yet to come to fruition. And this may be so. There is some suggestion that conglomerates are coming back into favor. Nevertheless, the theoretical arguments are heavily loaded against the conglomerates and the empirical evidence to date supports these arguments.

Many other empirical studies have been conducted on conglomerates, some of which contradict the results of those cited above. However, after a thorough examination of these studies, Canada's Royal Commission reached the conclusion that "Firms that have followed a strategy of conglomerate diversification have, in general, given their shareholders and given their investors below-average returns in the market."[22]

Section Three

Selling, Divesting, and Spinning-Off Companies

The basic decision rule to guide a director in determining whether the company should sell is:

SELL IF THE PREMIUM IS POSITIVE AND IS JUDGED TO BE THE BEST OBTAINABLE.

If the premium is positive then the shareholders of the selling company would be better off if the sale is made than if it is not. However, the first price may not be the best price, and a frequent negotiating tactic is to reject the first offer in order to obtain a higher one.

The Sell Decision Point

In most countries the Board of Directors' primary responsibility is to represent the interests of the shareholders; and it is important to consider the decision-making process that a director would follow, especially in the situation where the management opposes a takeover offer. The process is similar to that used in the buy situation.

It is first necessary to judge the actual price offered (Step 1). If cash is being offered then this is an easy matter; the price offered is the cash amount. However, if the acquiring company is offering its own shares, then it may well be that the price offered is not simply the current market value of the shares being offered. It could be that the acquiring company's shares are presently overvalued due to some bad news that is not reflected in their price. A takeover target should insist on a thorough examination of the acquiring company to make sure that there is no hidden bad news whose subsequent announcement would depress the price of the offered securities.

If the shares being offered are restricted, and if they

cannot be traded for several years, then they will be worth less than similar securities which can be freely traded. A 35 percent discount on the price of the offered shares, reflecting this lack of marketability, would be appropriate.[23]

In the closely held situation where the management is the owner, it is important to use a broad concept of price over and above the dollar value offered. It is necessary to consider employment agreements, noncompetes, perquisites, and so forth.

Having determined the actual price offered, the next step (Step 2) is to judge the stand-alone value of your company (the potential seller). This becomes a matter of judging whether the market value fairly represents the company's true value. Is the market undervaluing the company because of some major unannounced good news, such as a new invention or a lucrative contract, that is not reflected in the current market value of the firm? It is not enough to conclude that there has been no public announcement of such a thing; the market is able to deduce a lot of information that is not publicly announced, as in the case of the Australian nickel firm, cited earlier. The good news at the very least must be unique to the company. If it is common to other companies in the industry then more than likely the market price of the company's shares will already reflect the value of the industrywide good news.

On the other hand, it is possible that the target company's shares are overvalued by the market which means that the offered price premium is actually greater than it at first appears. If the company is widely recognized as a likely takeover target, then speculators will have bought the shares in anticipation of a high takeover offer and the shares will already be priced over and above the true underlying value of the firm.

Having developed a good idea of the price being offered for the company and the company's real value, the director can determine if the premium, the difference between the price offered and the stand-alone value, is indeed positive (Step 3).

The final step (Step 4) is to judge if the premium is the best obtainable, or if a higher one could be obtained through pursuing negotiating tactics, such as rejecting the initial offer. A particular problem is when the acquiring company is proposing to make an unfortunate acquisition from the viewpoint of its own shareholders, as in the case of a conglomerate purchase, and is offering its shares as payment. In this situation, its share price should be expected to drop as a direct result of the acquisition and the purchase should be structured so that the selling shareholders do not share in this loss, that all of the loss remains with the buying shareholders. This can be done by announcing the acquisition and waiting until the market has assimilated the news and adjusted the buying company's share price downwards before settling on the number of shares that must be paid. If the premium is positive and the best possible, a director has little latitude to vote against the takeover, if he represents the shareholders' interest. To vote against such an offer would be to the detriment of the company's shareholders.

Section IV provides an actual example of the above procedure, in which a Conoco director evaluates Du Pont's purchase offer and decides whether to support it.

Sell Strategies

Companies sometimes desire to sell—big companies seek to divest unattractive divisions, to slim down to manageable proportions, or to become understandable with a distinct image and destiny. Small entrepreneurial companies seek to sell out to a larger company. Perhaps the surest way of realizing considerable wealth is to sell out. The strategic question is where should a seller look in order to find a buyer who will offer the best possible price?

The company that can afford to pay the highest price is the company that has the greatest value-added. Seek first the horizontal buyer, the complements and competitors. Mr. Fred Braun, the owner of a manufacturer of special purpose tanks, Tec Tank, sought to sell out. The company he approached and subsequently sold to was Peabody International, because Peabody could use Tec Tank's product throughout its line and could afford a good price.

However a list of the logical buyers does not include everyone who may be willing to pay a good price. Some companies are "sugar daddies" who cannot really afford to pay healthy prices, not if they are interested in their own shareholders' welfare, but who nevertheless do. A would-be seller should not overlook this possibility. Sugar daddies are usually characterized by one of the following:

Foreigners. Foreigners recently have been the most generous sugar daddies. German companies, with the 1970s devaluation of the American dollar considered U.S. companies to be bargains and were willing to pay healthy prices. Likewise, United Kingdom companies have been reported to consider Australian companies attractive purchases. While local companies may appear to be cheap to foreigners when the purchase price is translated into their own currency, so too may the profits and dividends seem cheap when they are subsequently translated. When looking for a purchaser, remember foreigners.

Superior judges of worth. Some companies consider that the market is unsophisticated and that they can better judge the value of a company. Thus they may be willing to pay a considerably higher price than the market value because they believe the market has erred in its judgment as to the value of the company. A seller would approach such a company, explain away its low market value, and talk up its inherent unrecognized value.

The key question is how to find such a buyer. The disdain that some companies feel for the market can sometimes be deduced from their accounting policies. In the United States, if a company uses FIFO (first in first out) to value its inventory rather than LIFO (last in first out) then it is reporting higher earnings but paying more taxes, assuming that inflation will continue. The company may be saying in effect that the market puts more credence on accounting numbers than on real cash effects, that the market is unsophisticated. Empirical evidence on sophisticated markets indicates that such accounting policies will actually depress the market value, as logic would suggest, rather than increase the value.[24] One such company was Chrysler who in 1973 changed from LIFO to FIFO in order to report higher earnings, but also to pay higher taxes in the inflationary environment that prevailed. Occasionally a company will make public statements as to its valuation policy. One such instance was Northwest Industries, a conglomerate, that indicated that it used sophisticated discount cash flow techniques to pick undervalued acquisitions.[25] Such companies should be approached.

Earnings per share boosters. In reporting results, some companies attach much importance to their earnings per share. Such companies may seek to buy other companies with their stock and structure the purchase so that their earnings per share are boosted. These companies are of particular interest to would-be sellers, especially if the potential buyer has a high price-earnings ratio. This is because it can afford to pay any price multiple up to its own price-earnings ratio and still effect an increase in its earnings per share. And it can do this even if the price it pays is well in excess of the value of the acquired company and there is no value-added. For example, Company A, has the following characteristics:

Earnings	Shares outstanding	Earnings per share	Price-earnings ratio	Price per share	Market value
$1,000	1,000	$1.00	30	$30	$30,000

Company A is considering the acquisition of Company B (your company) which has the following characteristics:

	Shares	Earnings	Price-earnings	Price	Market
Earnings	outstanding	per share	ratio	per share	value
$300	100	$3.00	10	$30	$3,000

Company A has a price-earnings ratio of 30, considerably above the price-earnings ratio of Company B which is 10. Company A decides to pay a 100 percent premium for Company B, it pays 20 times earnings by issuing two of its own $30 shares (worth $60) for each $30 share of Company B. Company A issues 200 shares and now has 1,200 shares outstanding. Assume there is no value-added between the companies, that the earning streams just add together. The combined Company, A^1, will now report the following:

Earnings	Shares outstanding	Earnings per share
$1,300	1,200	$1.08

The earnings per share have increased from $1.00 to $1.08, a boost, and so Company A might well consider it has done well in acquiring Company B.

However if the market is sophisticated, recognizing that there is no value-added, it will value the combined company A^1 at the sum of the two separate companies, $33,000. This means that Company A^1, which now has issued a total of 1,200 shares, will have a price per share of $27.50, down from $30.00, and will have a price-earnings ratio of 25½, down from 30. Company A^1 will look as follows:

Earnings	Shares outstanding	Earnings per share	Price-earnings ratio	Price per share	Market value
$1,300	1,200	$1.08	25½	$27.50	$33,000

If the directors of Company A are operating in a sophisticated market and are interested in the welfare of their shareholders, they would not purchase Company B for twice what it is worth. Many companies, not realizing the above effect, use earnings per share criteria to determine the value of a target company, and such companies are fair game for would-be sellers. In a sophisticated market, earnings per share, whether or not an acquisition results in dilution, are irrelevant.

On the other hand, if the market is unsophisticated, it may well attribute A's price earnings ratio of 30 to B's earnings, $300, and so would increase the combined value to $39,000. Hence A's price per share would rise to $32.50, A would have won for its shareholders. This appeared to happen in the United States in the late 1960s during the early stages of the conglomerate boom, but the market soon realized what was happening and discounted the parent companies. Some maintain that the Australian markets operate in this unsophisticated manner.

It may be difficult to detect companies which use earnings per share criteria to value acquisitions. However, any would-be seller should list off those companies with a high price-earnings ratio which seem to place emphasis on their earnings per share in their annual reports. At very least, whenever talking to a potential buyer with a high price-earnings ratio, the would-be seller should always emphasize the favorable impact of the purchase on the buyer's earnings per share, thus improving the chances of obtaining a healthy price premium.

The highly leveraged (geared). Companies which have a high debt-to-equity ratio will compute their cost of capital at a low rate, reflecting that debt is cheaper than equity due to the tax deductibility of interest payments. A low cost of capital means that these companies may place a high present value on future earnings.

Thus any would-be seller who feels constrained to operate at a conservative debt-to-equity capital structure may well seek to sell to such a highly leveraged company. Finding such companies is a relatively easy matter involving nothing more than a search through annual reports.

The cash rich. Companies in mature markets tend to accumulate cash. And rather than return their cash to the shareholders by purchasing their own stock (and, in countries where this is disallowed, by paying extra dividends), the company may well be attracted to spending that excess cash in acquiring other companies, preferably companies which are growing and which need cash. A popular strategic concept of the mid-1970s was to consider the company as a portfolio of businesses and to seek to balance the cash generators with the cash users. Thus any growth company would seek out a cash rich mature company and offer itself as an acquisition.

Kennecott Copper, a copper producer, had about $800 million in cash and marketable securities as a result of its government-dictated divestiture of Peabody Coal. Reportedly, it sought to acquire another company in order to rid itself of the cash and thereby avoid being taken over itself. It acquired Carborundum, a maker of industrial abrasives, but hardly a growth company. Carborundum's market value was $280 million. Kennecott paid more than $560 million, thus dispensing with much of the excess cash. The companies were so dissimilar that there could be very little value-added from combining them. The market perceived this purchase as the wholesale pay out of the Kennecott cash to the shareholders of Carborundum, the wrong shareholders, and many stockholder suits threatened. In an effort to rationalize the acquisition, the then chief executive officer, Mr. Frank Milliken, pointed out that Kennecott was acquiring management talent. One executive search firm privately commented that it could have found a whole management team for Kennecott for a mere pittance in comparison to the $280 million premium paid and that their management team would have known something about copper! Any cash rich company is a ripe target for a would-be seller.

The shrinking company. Some companies are in businesses which are shrinking. A common response to such a situation is to diversify actively into other industries, especially those with attractive growth prospects. As mentioned earlier, R. J. Reynolds, a major producer of tobacco products feared the future of its market, and it actively sought to diversify by buying companies such as Sea-Land and Del Monte. R. J. Reynolds represented an attractive target during the 1970s to any would-be seller.

An extreme example of this situation is when a company is actually failing, and then it is clearly in the interests of the management to acquire quickly another company and so maintain their positions. However, it must be recognized that there may be a real economic cost if the company does not do this because the employee team might become demoralized and leave the company. The resulting inability to carry on business, even in the short term, may represent a cost to the shareholders which far exceeds the price premium paid for the company that is acquired.

Wildcat and star worshippers. In the United States a popular business strategy is the pursuit of market dominance. Companies are classified as wildcats (low market share in a high growth industry), stars (largest share, high growth industry), cash cows (largest share, low growth industry), or dogs (low share, low growth industry). Exponents of this strategic planning approach emphasize the attractiveness of being a star which can dominate a market, or a wildcat which could become a star. Many who follow this approach seek to acquire such companies. If anything, the concept has been oversold in the United States, and any business in a high growth market is probably overvalued by companies using this approach. Companies still using such a strategic planning approach should be targeted by high-growth, would-be sellers.

It is sometimes easy to detect companies using this strategic approach. Some describe the four different classifications and the strategic approach at great length in their publications or annual reports; Mead Corporation is one. Other companies following the market-dominance approach can only be detected by watching their actions in the marketplace. Such a company quickly seeks to build market share in a new industry, to dominate that position, and then to reap the rewards of that dominance.

Monument builders. Occasionally, the chief executive officer or managing director of a large and successful company may wish to be perceived in the annals of corporate history as the person who changed the direction of the company, the executive who set it on some great new course of growth. Utah International was seeking to sell to another corporation. It had a stand-alone market value of approximately $1,500 million. As discussed earlier, it sold to General Electric of U.S.A. for $2,000 million. Fortune Magazine examined the merger and concluded that there was little business rationale, that the merger was principally to satisfy the desire of Mr. Reginald Jones (the former chairman of General Electric) to create a "new G.E."[26] To find monument builders who have the power to act, start with the high profile company chiefs.

Investment banker clients. Some investment bankers seem to want a deal at any price. They advance several arguments to convince a buyer to pay an excessive price: "Open high or you'll leave room for another buyer to come in." This makes sense, but some buyers are overwhelmed by the tactical considerations and open at a price which is higher than the price at which they value the target company. Their shareholders would be better off if no deal is made; but the selling shareholders would prosper, at their expense. "You must pay a premium for control. The price per share on the stock exchange is for a small number of shares. A controlling block is worth more." Control may be necessary (but it may not be) to enable a buyer to effect the necessary interactions between the companies to realize value-added. But in and of itself, control has no pecuniary value to the buying shareholders. Control which does not result in interactions that give value-added is worthless. Where there will be value-added, demand some of it; where there will be no value-added, demand a premium for control. "The market value is the price agreed upon by a willing buyer and a willing seller. A new *market value* will be established." While the CEO of the buying company may be willing, he is not the real buyer. The shareholders are the real buyers, and they may not be so willing. The new and higher market value is of little relevance if the stock market does not validate it. Where there is no value-added, the evidence suggests that a sophisticated market will not validate an excessive price, and the buying company's shares will fall in value. Nevertheless, the buyer's advisor may be the seller's best friend, and the seller can help his cause by echoing some of the points that may be whispered in the buyer's ear.

Thus any would-be seller who is seeking the best possible price should make two lists of potential targets. The first list would be the complements and competitors, those companies who could logically afford to pay a high price because of the value-added that could result. The second list would be the sugar daddies, those companies who really cannot afford a high price but who may pay it nevertheless.

Spinning-Off Businesses

Spinning-off is a special form of buy/sell in which the buyers and the sellers are one and the same. A company which spins-off a business sets that business up as a separate corporation and issues the new stock to its current shareholders. A shareholder now has stock in two separate companies rather than in one. The basic rule to guide a director in determining whether a company should spin-off a business is:

SPIN-OFF IF THE COSTS OF BEING A PART OF THE PARENT EXCEED THE BENEFITS AND A DESIRABLE SALE CANNOT BE ARRANGED.

Conduct the following experiment. Take one subsidiary business and compare its situation with what would prevail if the business were a stand-alone company. What are the benefits and what are the costs that the business derives from being a part of your company?

If the costs exceed the benefits, then that business would be worth more as a stand-alone company. If this situation prevails throughout a large corporation we would have the extreme case where the stand-alone value that the parts would command as separate companies exceeds the value of the total combined company, where the sum of the parts exceeds the whole.

In a study of 20 oil companies, Donaldson, Lufken & Jenrette found that the companies were valued at an average of 55 percent of what they would have been valued at if they had been broken up into their component parts.[27] Such a discount represents a judgment by the capital markets that the costs of being a part of an integrated oil and gas organization exceed the benefits.

Having determined that a business should be spun-off, it should be recognized that this may not be the most desirable course of action for the shareholders. A preferred course is to sell the business to another party in order to obtain a price premium. With a spin-off situation, because the buyers and the sellers are one and the same, there is no premium. Management is very aware of another advantage to selling, namely, that the company can end up with cash to invest in the remaining operations. With a spin-off, no such cash infusion results; indeed, there is a temptation to sell at a bargain price to gain that cash. In this situation the shareholders would be better off with a spin-off, unless the cash investment in the company is sufficiently attractive to more than compensate for the bargain sale price. Hence the use of "desirable" sale in the decision rule. Only when no buyer can be found who will pay such a desirable price should a spin-off be considered.

As discussed earlier, Colgate-Palmolive, a manufacturer of soaps and detergents bought Helena Rubinstein, a cosmetics company, for $142 million. Some years later, after a series of reverses, Colgate-Palmolive sought to sell Helena Rubinstein. A tentative agreement was reached with a Japanese company to buy Helena Rubinstein for $75 million, but this fell through. One year later, Colgate-Palmolive had still not found a buyer, despite substantial effort. At this time, the management of Colgate-Palmolive would consider a spin-off.

There are several difficulties with spinning-off businesses. If a large company seeks to dismember itself completely into many small parts, to self-atomize, then the question always asked is what will happen to the headquarter staff? And this is a very real question for anyone at headquarters and subject to staff advice.

The second, and much more serious problem, is that of apportioning debt. When a large company borrows, the debt is usually secured by the total corporation. When seeking to dismember, the creditors will naturally demand a significant say as to how that debt will be split up between the components and how it is to be secured. It is this problem that probably prevented Colgate-Palmolive from spinning-off debt-ridden Helena Rubinstein. Helena Rubinstein was finally sold for about $20 million. The buyers were given a number of years to pay (with no interest charge) and Colgate-Palmolive did have to guarantee a substantial amount of debt. In the final analysis, Colgate-Palmolive may have sold Helena Rubinstein at a bargain price that was so low that the shareholders would have been better off with a spin-off.

What company should consider a spin-off strategy? Any large company made up of unrelated parts, irrespective of whether this was achieved by internal growth or by acquisitions, is a likely candidate. Being a part of such a company can sometimes offer little benefit but can be very expensive. The General Electric Co. Ltd. (GEC), Britain's dominant electrical and electronics company, sought to spin itself off into a number of separate companies. The *Economist*, noting that GEC's chief and founding father, Sir Arnold Weinstock, advocated the split, inquired why. It concluded:

- Technology— . . . Sir Arnold has always been eager to live down charges that he has failed to lead Britain's electronic industry into new technology as fast as he might have done . . .
- Management—With the group spanning a range of complex technologies, Sir Arnold worries that it is becoming impossible to manage it as closely as he would wish . . .
- Financial—the complexity of the GEC group tends to drag down its share price in relation to its earnings . . .

Thus the sum of the parts of GEC could well have a higher value than the whole today. That would be good news for shareholders, including Sir Arnold himself as he faces his old age.[28]

Any large corporation, even one which is predominantly within one business, should consider this strategy. With size, the costs of being a part increase and can increase to the point where they exceed the benefits. W. R. Grace was reported to have considered this strategy, at the prompting of security analysts.[29] IBM should consider a self-atomization policy in the interests of its shareholders, even though the U.S. government may drop its attempt to split IBM up into several smaller companies. It may be IBM's competitors who have most to fear from an IBM breakup. Several smaller companies may be tougher competition (and worth more) than the one monolith.

Section Four

The Evaluation of a Merger

Five groups of people are critically interested in evaluating the economic impact of a major merger. These are:

The directors of the buying company.
The directors of the selling company.
Security analysts.
The buying shareholders.
The selling shareholders.

We will consider the evaluation procedure for each.

Du Pont's Purchase of Conoco

We can illustrate the approaches by examining Du Pont's purchase of Conoco. This acquisition is particularly appropriate for our purposes for two reasons. It was a major acquisition and much public information was available about the lead up, rationale, price paid, and so forth. And it was not an obvious situation. Du Pont and Conoco were not as related as in a horizontal acquisition in which competitors merge, neither were they as unrelated as in a conglomerate acquisition in which complete strangers merge.

Dome Petroleum of Canada initiated the ultimate takeover of Conoco in May 1981. Dome was seeking Conoco's 53 percent interest in the Canadian company, Hudson Bay Oil and Gas, and in an attempt to force the sale tendered for 13 percent of Conoco's then outstanding stock which it then intended to swap for Conoco's Hudson Bay interest. Despite the Conoco's directors' opposition, over 50 percent of the Conoco stock was tendered and it became clear that Conoco itself was vulnerable as a takeover target. Dome's strategy was successsful. Conoco sold Dome its 53 percent of Hudson

Bay for the 22 million Conoco shares it had acquired, plus $245 million in cash. The Canadian distiller, Seagram, then entered the scene and became an aggressive bidder for 41 percent (and ultimately for 51 percent) of Conoco. Conoco sought a defensive merger with another U.S. oil company, Cities Service, but this fell through and Conoco turned to a white knight, Du Pont. Du Pont, a chemicals company, bid a higher price than Seagram, but Mobil Oil entered the fray with a higher price yet. Seagram, Du Pont, and Mobil progressively sweetened their offers to the shareholders of Conoco. The ultimate winner was Du Pont who offered more than Seagram but less than Mobil. The Mobil offer was not taken, presumably because of Conoco shareholders' fears that the government would stop Mobil's acquisition on antitrust grounds, and the apparent feeling that the additional premium being offered by Mobil was not sufficient to overcome this risk. Du Pont's final and winning offer was for $98 cash for 45 percent of Conoco's stock (39 million shares) and 1.7 Du Pont shares for each of the remaining 55 percent (an additional 48 million Conoco shares). At the time of its final offer, Du Pont's shares were trading at $45 5/8$, giving a total value to the offer of $7,550 million, or 87 per Conoco share. Prior to the takeover proceedings, Conoco was selling for 50 per share.

To illustrate the approach we will examine the evaluation process that each party should have followed, and we will make order-of-magnitude quantifications of the various benefits and costs of the acquisition. These quantifications will be indicative only, but in many acquisition situations even persons directly involved—especially the shareholders—have rather poor information, and order-of-magnitude numbers are the basis of a decision.

A Du Pont Director

The procedure that a director of a buying company should follow in determining whether he would recommend an acquisition was outlined in Section 2 under the heading, "The Buy Decision Point." The steps are:

Step 1: Estimate the offered price. The final offer by Du Pont was $7,550 million. Perhaps. A key question facing the Du Pont director was whether the Du Pont shares were indeed worth the 45⅝ market value, or were they worth more, giving a higher value to the offer? A Du Pont director would be privy to all significant inside information about the fortunes of Du Pont, some of which may not have been revealed to the markets nor deduced by external analysis. A temptation is to accept what most managers seem to believe, that their company is undervalued and that Du Pont's shares were worth more than 45⅝. If this was the case, then the offer for Conoco would be worth more than the $7,550 million. About the only grounds that a director would have to believe that the market valuation was low was if some positive information, such as the discovery of a significant new chemical or process, had not been announced to nor suspected by the market, or if the market for the company's share was quite unsophisticated. In the case of Du Pont, neither of these situations appears to have been the case. Du Pont is traded on the sophisticated New York Stock Exchange, and the directors would have insisted that any unannounced good news be made public during the bidding war. Apparently there was none.

The alternative situation can happen. If a company knows of some negative and significant information that is not yet reflected in the price of its shares, it may be tempted to issue its stock while it still commands a good price, to pay with "Chinese Money." Du Pont was wary of some developing situations, the entry of Saudi Arabia and of Exxon into chemicals, but these were well known to the investing public and Du Pont's share price would have reflected these factors already. In view of Du Pont's fine and ethical reputation, and the circumstances surrounding its invitation into the bidding for Conoco, it is quite unlikely that this second situation prevailed.

In the case of Du Pont, a director would most likely conclude that the value of the Du Pont shares was the current market value, 45⅝, and that the value of the offer was $7,550 million.

Step 2: Estimate Conoco's stand-alone value. One of the rationales offered by Du Pont's chairman, Mr. Edward G. Jefferson, was that "it's an opportunity to obtain a strong natural-resource asset position at a substantial discount."[30] In other words, Conoco was a bargain that was worth considerably more than its current market value. The market was wrong.

When faced with this assertion, a director should carefully examine a target company's share market by considering each of the factors that determines the ability of the company's market to value its shares correctly. Considering the market for Conoco's shares:

Information policy. Conoco was not unduly secretive about its prospects. The market received a normal flow of information from management.

External information. Conoco was followed by a

team of security analysts; any external environmental factors, and factors common to other oil companies, were well understood and accounted for.

Multibusinesses. Conoco was made up of two principal parts; a vertically integrated oil and gas business, and a coal business. Thus the market would have had some difficulty in assessing Conoco's value, and it would probably have suffered a discount as a result. However this discount could not be considered the basis of a bargain price unless Du Pont planned to break up and sell off Conoco's several parts and thereby simplify the market's assessment of Conoco's future. The business press speculated that Du Pont would sell off Conoco's coal interests to retire the debt incurred to make the acquisition, although Mr. Jefferson indicated at that time that this was not the plan.[31] Nevertheless, assuming that this would indeed be the strategy, then it would be reasonable to assume that Conoco was suffering a discount which it would not suffer after the acquisition and split up. The data contained in Canada's Royal Commission on Corporate Concentration suggest that this discount would be less than six percent. For our purposes, a three percent discount is a reasonable measure.[32] The fact that Du Pont will become more complex and suffer a multibusiness discount itself will be considered when the costs of the acquisition are examined.

Popularity. At the time of the acquisition, the whole oil industry had recently suffered a substantial drop in the value of its shares, a result of the oil glut and downward pressure on oil company profits. The question is whether this was an inappropriate and emotional down adjustment, or whether it was in line with the realities of the situation. The author's judgment is that oil companies were not being discounted unreasonably. Only a very self-confident (foolhardy?) person could conclude otherwise with such a well-known and established industry.

Shareholder following. Conoco was actively followed by institutions which owned 62 percent of the 87 million shares outstanding.[33] Institutions typically invest in a rational manner, and their buy-sell decisions are backed with careful research.

Trading activity. Conoco's stock was well traded. Its market was not thin.

Market size, country development, and customs. Conoco was traded on the New York Stock Exchange, perhaps the most sophisticated of all markets.

Having considered each of these factors, a director would be forced to conclude that the market for Conoco's stock was a good one, that it more than likely accurately valued the company's prospects, and that to assume Conoco was a bargain would be hopeful. More likely, the opposite situation would be of more concern, that the Conoco price had moved up to 50 in anticipation of a takeover. An analysis of Conoco share trades would not suggest that insider trading had pushed the price of Conoco shares up prior to the announcement of the initial Dome tender offer. Reportedly, the Dome offer was unwanted and came as a complete surprise. Conoco's shares were actually falling prior to the offer. Thus the stand-alone value of Conoco would be judged to be 50 per share, the price prior to the Dome tender offer. Admittedly, Conoco had sold off its Hudson Bay assets subsequent to this pretender condition, but it had received a reasonable price (although less than Conoco had at first thought it worth).[34] In summary, a three percent revaluation would be appropriate to account for the fact that Conoco was a multibusiness which would have suffered a price discount and that Du Pont would probably split it up and sell off the coal business. Thus a Du Pont director would judge Conoco's stand-alone value to be $4,481 million, as outlined in Table 2 on page 100.

Step 3: Determine the price premium. The premium is the difference between the final offer price, $7,550 million, and Conoco's stand-alone value estimated at $4,481 million, or $3,069 million. This premium will now be compared with an estimate of the value-added that results from combining Du Pont and Conoco.

Step 4: Estimate the value-added. As a general rule, the value of a benefit or a cost can be judged by considering the normal price earnings ratio of the company. If a company has a P/E ratio of eight, and if the change in annual aftertax earnings from a benefit or cost is estimated at $1 million, then a first estimate of the impact of this projected earnings change, using the multiple of eight, is a change in market value of $8 million. However, recognition must be given to the degree of risk and to the timing of the projected earnings change; usually a lesser multiple is selected. Table 1 gives an indication of how this multiple may be adjusted for the timing and risk. Thus if the $1 million aftertax change in annual earnings is uncertain and will take several years to be realized, then the impact would be judged at $2.4 million ($1 million times 8 times 30 percent).

Table 1
Price-earnings multiple adjustment

	Risk		
	Certain	Likely	Uncertain
Timing			
Immediate..........	90%	70	50
Short-term (2-3 years)	70	50	30
Long-term (5 plus years)	50	30	10

This is an approximate method only. Different earning streams attract different multiples in the market, due to their different natures. This method assumes that the benefit or cost is similar to the underlying business whose P/E ratio was selected as the beginning point. It is the selection of the wrong P/E ratio that is the basis of the fallacious earnings per share dilution technique, discussed earlier, that some use to value companies. An analyst who is privy to a detailed projection of the benefit or cost would use a technique such as discounted cash flow to judge its impact on the company's market value.

The Operational Benefits:

Sales and marketing. No interaction was claimed between Conoco and Du Pont that would result in any direct sales or marketing benefits.

Costs and production. A rationale offered for the merger by Du Pont's chairman was that the merger would "make Du Pont more competitive internationally . . . big oil companies, such as Exxon Corporation, and Middle East oil-producing countries are increasingly moving into the chemical business."[35] In other words, the merger was seen as a means of maintaining Du Pont's competitiveness, of ensuring the continued access to feedstocks at a competitive price. Reputedly, access to feedstocks has long been a concern for Du Pont's management. Whether the investment community was as concerned is quite another matter. It could be argued that this glut would worsen as Iran and Iraq recover to their prewar production levels and as new oil discoveries come on stream, and that the vast quantities of recently discovered domestic U.S. gas would be displacing imported oil. However let us give the benefit of the doubt; let us assume that Du Pont shares have indeed been selling at a discount as a result of this potential feed stock situation, and that the acquisition of Conoco will result in a recovery in Du Pont's share price by as much as 15 percent.

Research and technology. Du Pont's chairman claimed that Conoco will benefit from Du Pont's research, technical, and engineering strength in such areas as improved tertiary recovery of crude oil and coal-conversion technology.[36] While this may well be true, it must be pointed out that Conoco has had its successes in research.[37]

However, assume that this technological benefit will result in an enormous 20 percent increase in aftertax earnings within five years. Conoco's earnings were approximately $1,000 million after tax per year. The increase would be $200 million per year. Conoco's premerger P/E was 6 and the timing and uncertainty of this benefit suggest a factor of between 10 and 30 percent (Table 1). Thus the impact is estimated at $240 million ($200 million times 6 times 20 percent).

Resources. No apparent gain.

Managerial. It was claimed that Du Pont is a more tightly managed company than Conoco.[38] Assume a resulting increase in Conoco's aftertax earnings of 10 percent, $100 million, within five years. Considering the uncertainty and the timing, an increase of $120 million is an appropriate measure of the impact on Conoco's value ($100 million times the P/E of 6 times 20 percent from Table 1).

The Nonoperational Benefits:

Funding. The market's reaction to the acquisition was to lower Du Pont's credit rating from AAA to AA, making new debt more expensive for Du Pont, a negative benefit. But this would have a minimal effect on values. Zero value-added.

Taxes. Du Pont will borrow approximately $4,000 million to finance its new acquisition, changing its capital structure from a rather conservative 21 percent debt to a more typical 40 percent debt structure. Because of the tax subsidy inherent in debt (due to the tax deductibility of interest payments) this could be considered a benefit giving up to $2,000 million of additional value. However, Du Pont's chairman has indicated that he intends to go to work to whittle the huge $4 billion debt Du Pont is incurring to acquire Conoco.[39] This ties with the earlier assumption of selling off Conoco's coal assets. Assume that Du Pont will not maintain the more optimal capital structure, zero value-added.

However there could be a substantial benefit from an increase in the depletion allowance. By attributing much of the purchase price to Conoco's oil fields, their tax basis can be raised and the depletion allowance increased, resulting in lower taxes on Conoco's profits. A detailed study would be necessary to estimate this gain, but assuming an increase of $1 billion in the basis of Conoco's fields, this could result in an additional depletion allowance of $100 million per year, to reduce taxes by $50 million per year and so provide a gain of $50 million after tax per year in "real" earnings.[40] Recognizing the immediacy and certainty of this gain, an estimate of the increase in market value is $270 million ($50 million times the P/E of 6 times 90 percent from Table I).

Risk. Chairman Jefferson maintained that "if prices are rising at the crude-oil level then it becomes difficult to raise the prices of (Du Pont's) downstream products (which use oil as a raw material). As soon as you have a crude-oil position you're insulated from that. The fact that you lost a little downstream is protected by what you have upstream."[41] In other words, Conoco will give Du Pont an oil hedge; it will protect Du Pont's profits from future oil price rises (and reduce the benefit from any future fall in oil prices). From the point of view of Du Pont's shareholders, Du Pont is already valued as a part of a well-diversified portfolio. Presumably Du Pont's shareholders would participate elsewhere in any such increases (or decreases) in oil prices. Thus this is no additional benefit to shareholders (they already have it) and Du Pont's share price should not be expected to appreciate as a result. Zero value-added.

Familial. Conoco does not give Du Pont an entry to any closed international markets, nor vice-versa.

The Costs of the Acquisition:

Front end. Investment bankers and legal fees will

cost the combined companies in the order of $30 million, $15 million after tax assuming they are expensed.

Direct ongoing. No additional expenses would be expected.

Managerial. Conoco's management did not want to be acquired. While Du Pont was invited to tender, Conoco's management was making the best of what they considered a bad situation. Du Pont should expect to lose some key Conoco managers, resulting in a decrease in value. But let us assume that this is negligible.

Learning costs. Du Pont intends to minimize any management changeovers and to leave Conoco as a separate subsidiary. However, at some stage Du Pont should be expected to make some significant changes and become intimately involved in Conoco's affairs, requests for capital, strategic plans, and so forth. We should expect Du Pont to incur at least some learning costs. Assume that this is 2.5 percent of Conoco's value.

Opportunity. And while it makes these changes Du Pont itself should expect some loss of value as it focuses its efforts on Conoco. But assume that this is negligible.

Multibusiness discount. Du Pont will become a more complicated company and more difficult for the market to value, even if Conoco's coal assets are sold off. The effect of this will be to cause a discount. One analyst expressed disappointment when observing that Du Pont "becomes this huge company that is more than half natural resources and the specialty divisions of Du Pont are getting lost."[42] Assume that three percent of the combined Du Pont/Conoco value (see the earlier discussion as to the value of this discount) is appropriate.[43]

Thus a generous assessment of the total value-added resulting from the merger is in the order of $1,217 million, as tabulated in Table 2.

Step 5: Compare the value-added with the premium. The value-added of $1,217 million is less than the $3,069 million premium. Thus a director would vote against a proposed purchase of Conoco's shares, in the interests of Du Pont's shareholders. The complete analysis is shown in Table 2. This table provides an evaluation format which can be used by a director in any buying situation.

In making this assessment, the intent was to be kind to the Du Pont directors and to give the most favorable reasonable estimate of value-added in an attempt to justify their vote for the acquisition. In actual fact, their decision was probably worse for their shareholders than the above analysis indicates. Managerial and opportunity costs were given zero values, but these can be significant. Admittedly, numbers were plucked from the air, but such order-of-magnitude numbers will give a clearer indication of how a director should vote than will "gut feel" which is the usual alternative in the hurried white knight role that Du Pont found itself.

A Conoco Director

The procedure that a director of a selling company would follow to judge if he was in favor of a sell-out was outlined in Section 3 under the heading, "The Sell Decision Point." The procedure is:

Step 1: Estimate the offered purchase price. A Conoco director would first judge the value of the Du Pont offer: $3,822 million in cash plus 82 million Du Pont shares selling at 45⅝ each at the time of the final

Table 2
The Du Pont director's decision ($ millions)

	Totals
Step 1: Estimate the offered purchase price	
39 million shares at 98, plus 48 million shares at 1.7 Du Pont shares (82 million at 45⅝ each)	$7,550
Step 2: Estimate Conoco's stand-alone value	
87 million shares at 50 per share	4,350
Multibusiness revaluation of 3 percent	131
	$4,481
Step 3: Determine the price premium	$3,069
Step 4: Estimate the value-added	
Operational benefits	
Sales and marketing	—
Costs and production—15 percent of Du Pont (156 million shares at 45⅝)	1,068
Research and technology—$200 by 6 by 20 percent	240
Resources	—
Managerial—$100 by 6 by 20 percent	120
Nonoperational benefits	
Funding	—
Taxes—$50 by 6 by 90 percent	270
Risk	—
Familial	—
Costs	
Front-end	(15)
Direct ongoing	—
Managerial	—
Learning—2.5 percent of $4,350	(109)
Opportunity	—
Multibusiness discount—3 percent of the combined companies	(357)
	$1,217
Step 5: Compare the value-added with the premium. The value-added, $1,217 is less than the price premium, $3,069. Vote *against* the acquisition of Conoco.	

offer. A director would be concerned that the market value for Du Pont's shares did not reflect some bad news about Du Pont that was not public knowledge. The director would insist on a thorough "due diligence" meeting between the Conoco and Du Pont managements in which any such negative factors would be unearthed. Assume that there were no such negative factors, that the market value was reasonable, that Du Pont's shares were worth 45⅝, and that the offer was worth $7,550 million, or 87 per Conoco share.

Step 2: Estimate Conoco's stand-alone value. The Conoco director would then assess whether Conoco was selling at an unwarranted discount. By the time of Du Pont's final offer, August 4, 1981, Conoco had announced second quarter earnings that were down 36 percent from the prior year, after excluding extraordinary gains.[44] A Conoco director certainly had grounds to believe that the low 50 per share market value was reasonable. The usual temptation in this circumstance would be to believe that the market was wrong and that Conoco was worth far more than 50 per share, or $4,350 million. But recognizing the sophistication of the market for Conoco shares, one would be hard pressed to believe that it had erred significantly and that Conoco's value was not close to $4,350 million.

Step 3: Determine if the price premium is positive. The premium is the difference between the $7,550 million offer and the $4,350 million stand-alone value, a premium of $3,200 million, or 73 percent. This is positive and clearly a handsome gain for Conoco's shareholders.

Step 4: Judge if this is the best offer. The final step for the Conoco director is to judge if Du Pont's offer was the best obtainable. Recognizing that there had been a bidding war for Conoco, the directors would have felt assured that they were indeed obtaining a good price, if not the best. Whether the Du Pont bid was better than the Mobil bid involves an assessment of the antitrust risks versus the additional premium ($1,350 million more than Du Pont's) that Mobil offered. There is another factor other than the antitrust risks in this assessment. If Du Pont's offer was too attractive, if the premium exceeded the value-added, then the value of Du Pont's shares should be expected to drop, and the premium would be less than the $3,200 figure estimated in Step 3, because the Conoco shareholders were to receive part payment in Du Pont shares. A Conoco director would surely have suspected that this was indeed the case. On the other hand, Mobil would be more likely to generate appreciable value-added being more closely related to Conoco, and Mobil offered part payment in senior securities. Thus there would be less decay in the Mobil premium. Nevertheless, the antitrust risk was great and it is felt that the conclusion was reasonable: that Du Pont's offer was the better. Thus a director for Conoco could well recommend that the shareholders accept the Du Pont offer. The Conoco shareholders agreed with this assessment and took the Du Pont offer.

A Security Analyst

The situation for a security analyst is different from that of a director. His task is to judge the market's response and the resulting share price, rather than to make a yea/nay decision as in the case of the director. His question is one of how much.

To judge the impact of an acquisition, an analyst looks at the total components of value in the resulting firm, the number of shares outstanding, and then assesses the expected price per share. The procedure is (1) estimate the buying company's pretender stand-alone value, (2) estimate and add the selling company's stand-alone value, (3) estimate and add the value-added that will result, (4) subtract any cash payouts to the selling shareholders, to give (5) the total value of the resulting combined company. Then (6) compute the number of shares that will be outstanding, taking into account any shares issued to the selling shareholders, and finally (7) compute the price per share which is the total value divided by the number of shares outstanding. Table 3 shows the above steps, giving an estimated Du Pont share price of 38.28.

However there is a bigger issue than just this one acquisition, and that is the message concerning future acquisitions. Du Pont had traditionally been a very conservative company. A former Du Pont chief executive commented, "Running a conglomerate is a job for management geniuses, not ordinary mortals like us at Du Pont."[45] (Mr. Jefferson would probably retort that Conoco represents a vertical integration, not a conglomerate acquisition. But Conoco and Du Pont are so different that it may as well be thought of as a conglomerate acquisition when considering the management skills required to run the resulting company.) This acquisition clearly demonstrates a dramatic change under the leadership of the new chairman. Du Pont should be expected to make aggressive diversifying acquisitions elsewhere, finances permitting, and security analysts should expect that these too will be detrimental to the existing shareholders. Du Pont officials have expressed their intention to enter new fields such as pharmaceuticals. Thus the price per share of Du Pont under this leadership should be expected to drop in the near term

Table 3
Value of postacquisition Du Pont shares

		Totals (millions)
Step 1:	Estimate Du Pont's stand-alone value 156 million shares at 46⅜ per share (the pretender value)	$7,235
Step 2:	Estimate Conoco's stand-alone value See Table 2	4,481
Step 3:	Estimate the value-added See Table 2	1,217
Step 4:	Subtract any cash payout 39 million shares at 98 per share	(3,822)
Step 5:	Compute the total value	$9,111
Step 6:	Compute the number of shares outstanding Du Pont's shareholders	156
	Issued to Conoco's shareholders (48 million by 1.7)	82
		238
Step 7:	Compute the price per share $9,111 million divided by 238 million	$38.28
Step 8:	Judge the implications for future acquisitions	$35.00

below the 38.28 value estimated, to say, 35, in anticipation of future bloodlettings.

Taking account of this purchase of Conoco and what it portends of future forays by Du Pont, a security analyst would recommend that investors sell their Du Pont shares in anticipation of a price decline in the near future to the mid 30s.

Will Du Pont's shares actually fall to the mid 30s? Naturally, account must be taken of total market movements and any changes in Du Pont's environment or strategy. But even if there are no such changes, there is a 50/50 chance that Conoco was overvalued by the stock market and that Du Pont's shares will drop still lower. There is also a 50/50 chance that Conoco was undervalued, in which case the price will not fall as low. There is only a small chance, when you consider the size of the premium that was paid, that the Du Pont shareholders will actually win and the price of Du Pont shares rise as a result of the acquisition.

The Conoco Shareholders

At first flush, the Conoco shareholders may well have believed that they were being paid a significant price premium, and indeed they were, however, not as much as at first expected. The reason is that they accepted a predetermined number of Du Pont shares and as the market reacts to the Du Pont acquisition, the Du Pont shares should be expected to drop in value, which the Conoco shareholders will also suffer. Thus, rather than receiving $7,550 million and a premium of $3,200 million which were figured at the Du Pont share price of 45⅝, they would receive $6,692 million and a reduced premium of $2,342 million, assuming that Du Pont's shares do fall to 35 per share. This is considerably less, but a healthy premium nevertheless, and the Conoco shareholders have clearly won. They were wise to vote for the sale to Du Pont.

The Du Pont Shareholders

The Du Pont shareholders have lost; wealth has been transferred from them to the Conoco shareholders. The amount of this transfer is the anticipated fall in share price from the pretender 46⅜ per share down to the 38.28 that results. Thus the transfer from the Du Pont shareholders, holding 156 million shares, is $1,263 million. The total loss to Du Pont shareholders should be expected to be still greater, considering the strategic import of the acquisition.[46] The shareholders should not have accepted their directors' recommendation to buy Conoco. The drop in Du Pont's share price before the final decision indicates that many did not, and the response was to sell off their Du Pont holdings before the price worsened further.

In summary, Du Pont's purchase of Conoco was an unfortunate recommendation on the part of the Du Pont's directors which should be expected to result in a loss of wealth by Du Pont's shareholders. There is only an outside chance that they will win. It was a fortunate recommendation by the Conoco directors for the Conoco shareholders, although it could have been better yet if the Du Pont share price was allowed to fall before the number of shares was finally settled upon. From the viewpoint of security analysts and investors, this acquisition and the strategy it implies, suggest that Du Pont shares should fall to the mid 30s in the near future.

One last point is worthy of thought. Du Pont could afford and did obtain the best advice possible. Reportedly they paid about $15 million to their investment banker, First Boston Corp., who advised them throughout.[47] What went wrong? First Boston's credentials are impeccable. Presumably they were asked *how* it should be done but not the bigger question, *should* it be done? That second question is the domain of the directors, and is one surely that no director would ask any investment banker, not when there is a $15 million incentive to answer in the affirmative. If an answer to the "how to" question costs $15 million, what would an answer to the bigger "should we" question cost? Perhaps directors are underpaid and investment bankers are overpaid.

Conclusions

Buyers

An acquisition can result in one of four situations for the buying shareholders. These are:

1. Win/Win: In this happiest of all scenarios a company makes a bargain-priced acquisition and is able to develop value-added. A company is worth $100; it is bought for $80. The buyer develops value-added of $50 and the acquired company is now worth $150. The buyer and its shareholders have won by $20, the bargain discount, plus $50, the value-added. This is the Shearson Loeb Rhoades acquisition strategy.

2. Win: This is where the value-added exceeds the price premium. It can be achieved with one of two strategies. First, the pursuit of value-added, in which a company worth $100 is acquired for $150. The buyer develops value-added of $70 and the acquired company is now worth $170. The buyer and its shareholders are ahead by $20. This is the Motorola/Codex acquisition. Alternatively, the strategy could be the pursuit of bargains. A company worth $100 is acquired for $80. There is no value-added, the company is still worth $100. The buyer and its shareholders have won by $20. This, reputedly, is the Beatrice strategy.

3. Lose: This is the circumstance in which the value-added is less than the premium. The buying company does not realize sufficient value-added to cover the price premium. This is the Du Pont/Conoco acquisition. Alternatively, the buying company damages the company it acquires and it realizes value-lost which exceeds the bargain discount. This may be the actual Beatrice situation, at least with some of its acquisitions.

4. Lose/Lose: This is the worst scenario, the typical conglomerate one. A company is worth $100; it is acquired for $150. The buyer realizes value-lost, the company's value drops to $80. The buyer and its shareholders have lost by the $50 premium plus the $20 value-lost. This is the Colgate-Palmolive/Helena Rubinstein acquisition.

Small companies have an opportunity for great growth using the acquisition route. They are the most likely to achieve the first scenario, win/win, or the second, win. There are two reasons for this. Small companies typically buy small companies which are often closely held and hence more likely to be bargains. As well, they are not constrained by antitrust considerations; they can buy competitors which permits the generation of significant value-added. Every small company should consider an aggressive acquisition program as a growth strategy.

The situation is not so fortunate for large companies. The majority of acquisitions by large companies are detrimental to their shareholders. If one large company acquires another large company, it will almost certainly pay a significant price premium, but will have little chance to develop significant value-added. This is because the two companies are usually too dissimilar to enable the generation of significant value-added. If they were sufficiently similar, the merger would never have been allowed by the antitrust authorities. As well, large companies are usually complete; they do not have glaring weaknesses which could be overcome as a result of a merger thus creating significant value-added. The usual situation when one large company buys another is the third situation, lose. Alternatively, if a large company buys a small one and then plays an active role in its operations, the costs often exceed any benefits. The buyer pays a premium, and then suffers value-lost. This is the fourth situation, lose/lose.

It is an unusual large company that wins for its shareholders at the acquisition game. One possibility that a large company has of winning is to operate on a small scale, seeking value-added by acquiring product lines to add to its own, or seeking closely held companies at bargain prices. In either case, one particular acquisition is so small relative to the buying company that many large companies feel that it is not worth doing. The solution, perhaps, is to decentralize the acquisition function in a large corporation and to make many small acquisitions. This could result in significant value-added.

Sellers

Selling shareholders almost always win. If a company is publicly traded, its share value can be observed, and the shareholders are almost certain to receive a premium above this. Even if the shareholders of a closely held company do not receive a premium above the company's value, there are often nonpecuniary returns to the sellers that make it worthwhile to sell at a lower price. The sellers win despite what might appear to be a bargain price.

The selling shareholders can lose in several ways. The company may be unaware of its value, or it may be underrepresented during negotiations. Competent advice would prevent this. Alternatively, the sellers could take equity securities as payment, and these could drop in value, making the price a bargain. A seller who accepts shares must be thorough in the due diligence process and must recognize the risk inherent in this form of payment.

Postscript:

A Broader Perspective

A corporation is a creature of society, and the justification for its existence is its efficient delivery of the goods and services that society requires. In considering the buying or selling of companies, we need to extend our scope beyond what is good for shareholders to what is good for society as a whole. Is the buying or selling of companies an activity that society should condone or even encourage? This is a concern that many a director feels.

Society's Interests

We have been considering how a corporation should act in order to maximize the wealth of its shareholders, which becomes a question of how to maximize the corporation's current market value. This is good for shareholders, but we need to look at the effect on society as a whole.

At first blush, maximizing the current market value seems to be a shortsighted and narrow goal, hardly an appropriate one for a socially conscious corporation. But we must look further.

A company maximizes its current market value by maximizing the present value of all future economic earnings. If a corporation were to ignore some trend in its product market that will impact in the future, then it should expect its market value to fall, now. The market value of a corporation responds today to future prospects. Shortsighted actions which are taken to give a short-term boost, at the expense of the long term, usually depress the current market value of a corporation. Maximization of current market value requires a long-term perspective.

The second initial reaction is that concern for shareholders only is too narrow. If a corporation was to ride roughshod over its employees, lowering morale and raising turnover, the corporation should expect its long-term profitability and hence its current market value to be depressed. If the corporation was to ignore its customers and not focus on serving them in a competitive manner, then it would lose out to its competitors, and again its long-term profitability and its current value would be depressed. If a corporation was to ignore some strongly felt societal value and was, for example, to spew pollution into the environment, then it would suffer the consequences of such actions. Legal measures by the state and social pressures would depress profitability and lower the current market value. A concern for the current market value of the corporation is not as narrow and shortsighted as it at first appears. It requires a long-term and broad perspective.

We can go beyond considering market value in general. We can look at the specific instance of two companies merging. We placed much emphasis on measuring the value-added from the point of view of shareholders, but we need to consider the value-added from the point of view of society.

Reviewing the benefit and cost components of value-added, we can see that, for the most part, what is beneficial or costly to the shareholders is also beneficial or costly to society. Society benefits when goods and services are more effectively generated and distributed, when they are produced for less, when better use is made of technology, when resources are more fully utilized, and when better management techniques are adopted. Society is also better served if the most deserving companies achieve financing, if companies are able to select the better investments, if risk can be more effectively handled and managed, and if nationalistic interests are satisfied.

On the cost side, expensive front-end costs mean that society has many people involved, diverted from other productive functions. Higher direct costs are largely a measure of the extra compensation that people demand for working in a less desirable environment. Loss of experienced management, that is, managerial costs, means that the company will be less able to serve society. Society also suffers while new management learns its lessons in a new business and if that management ignores its traditional business while doing so. And uncertainty as to what a corporation is doing, the root of the multibusiness discount, is a loss to society too.

For the most part there is a reasonable correlation between what is good or bad for shareholders and what is good and bad for society, and between the value-added from the shareholders' viewpoint and the *value-added* from society's. However, four specific areas where there can be a considerable difference need to be examined carefully.

1. Competitive and market power. If a horizontal strategy is pursued, there will be value-added for shareholders and for society as companies combine into more efficient units. But only up to a point. It is possible for the industry to become so concentrated that the remaining firms earn excessive profits, and they are able to charge high prices due to a lack of competition. Thus while the monopoly or oligopoly lasts, there will be a transfer of wealth from society to the shareholders. Over the long run there will be a tendency for the companies to be less innovative than they might otherwise have been, with a resulting loss to society of new and better products. Ultimately, this situation will be rectified with the arrival of new entrants to the market or with substitute products, but this will take time. Some govenments legislate against such mergers.

A company with many component businesses could indulge in predatory pricing in which the company deliberately charges unrealistically low prices in one product market in order to weaken and even eliminate the competition. It could charge these low prices by using its other businesses for temporary support. With the reduction of competition that results, the company could then raise its prices to excessive levels and effect a transfer of wealth from society to its shareholders.

A commonly cited advantage of the large company is its ability to force suppliers to accept artificially low prices. This results in a transfer of wealth from the shareholders of the supplying company to the shareholders of the purchasing company. It is questionable if this is a legitimate area of concern for society as a whole as it is a private dealing between two parties. Society would be hurt if the supply companies were forced into bankruptcy, but this would not be in the interests of the purchasing company either.

Thus in the competitive area, there is clearly the possibility of a significant misalignment between what is good for shareholders and what is good for society as a whole.

2. Concentrated control. Combining companies results in concentrated control. People dislike this. There is a feeling of resentment within society when people no longer know with whom they are doing business; and there is fear that all economic activity will be controlled by a few unknown presidents at a few unheard of corporate headquarters. It is not necessary that this power be abused to be offensive; its mere existence is odious.

To say that the purchase of a company's product is a vote for that company is misleading in this particular circumstance. The purchase of Dannon Yogurt is a vote for the yogurt, its taste, its price, for its "No Artificial Anything" claim. It is not a vote for Mr. Rasmussen's control of many companies in many sectors of the society (Mr. Rasmussen was chief executive officer of Beatrice Foods, which owned Dannon). If that issue were put to the same consumers who voted for (bought) Dannon Yogurt, it would be soundly defeated.

Corporate managements deplore the antibusiness sentiment that is found so often in today's newspapers, magazines, and television programs. But they should recognize that such sentiments are almost invariably directed toward big corporations whose size is so often no longer a source of benefit to society. It is the big company that provides the grist for the antifree enterprise mill. It is not the small local operation whose owners are known. When it comes to defending the free enterprise system, large corporations appear to be their own worst enemies.

3. Dislocations and unemployment. A frequently cited undesirable consequence of a merger is that the new corporate owner is likely to close or move plants, throwing many employees out of work. There is considerable human suffering caused by these corporate maneuvers, and this suffering is unevenly spread throughout society. The person who loses his job suffers acutely. It is no wonder that politicians are very cognizant of this cost and often demand assurances that this will not happen.

However, this is the nature of the free enterprise system. While there can indeed be short-term suffering that is inequitably spread, the long-term benefits are enormous. Without this economic process we would all today be suffering from the inefficiencies of firms and plants that should have long since been (and actually were) closed. Essentially, we have a trade-off between the short-term costs suffered by displaced employees and their families and the long-term benefits that accrue to all of society.

4. Taxation. One of the ways of adding value for shareholders is to reduce the taxes paid to the government, to society generally. More for shareholders, less for society.

Society, through the government, has decided to provide such features as tax loss carry forwards, presumably because it judges that it gains in the long run. By sharing the risks with the shareholders, shareholders will be encouraged to make investments in productive assets, and this is to society's benefit. Presumably, because governments can and do change their taxation policies, the current policy represents a collective judgment as to the optimal taxation situation at the time.

Of the four areas of potential disparity between the interests of shareholders and of society as a whole, two were found to be potentially troublesome. These were market power in which market abuses are beneficial to shareholders but detrimental to society, and concentrated control which is odious to society and of little benefit in and of itself to shareholders.

The Decision Criteria Revisited

The directors of a company have a legitimate concern for the public good. Ultimately it is in the interests of the company, and of the whole free enterprise system, that directors do have this concern. In the final analysis, concern for society's interests can be considered a concern for one's self-interest.

The Buy Situation

We have developed three decision rules for buying, selling, and spinning-off companies, and will now examine whether these should be modified to take account of the greater interests of society. The first rule for buying companies was:

BUY IF THE VALUE-ADDED EXCEEDS
THE PRICE PREMIUM.

This is a decision rule which guides a director in acting in the interests of his company's shareholders. From the viewpoint of society the decision rule would be:

BUY IF THE *VALUE-ADDED* IS POSITIVE

where *value-added* is the additional value to society as a whole, as distinct from that to shareholders and the capital markets. In other words, if any value from the point of view of society results, then it is in society's interests that the acquisition be made.

In comparing the two decision rules it should be recognized that the value-added to society, *value-added*, may be less than that to the shareholders of the company because of the possibility of market power benefits to shareholders which are a cost to society, and because of the possibility of concentrated control which is also a cost to society.

However, there is a second aspect to consider. While the value-added to the shareholders may be greater than to society, the criterion for shareholders is more stringent. For shareholders the value-added must exceed the premium to be paid; for society the *value-added* need only be positive. Thus while the *value-added* is potentially less for society, society has a built-in protection because of this more stringent criterion for judging whether a possible combination is good.

For the most part, any disparity between what is good for the shareholders and what is good for society is more than covered by the more stringent criterion, at least where there is an effective antitrust policy. Directors usually need not worry about society's interests. If a combination is good for shareholders, it is likely to be very good for society. If there is not an effective antitrust policy, a director may well be concerned with the cost to society of excessive market power that may result from a merger.

The Sell Situation

The decision rule for selling a company was:

SELL IF THE PREMIUM IS POSITIVE AND IS JUDGED TO BE THE BEST OBTAINABLE.

This decision criterion at first appears irrelevant to society. If a merger is good for the buying shareholders, it is good for society too, and society has no interest in the actual price or transfer of wealth between the buying and selling shareholders.

However, if a company receives an attractive sell offer with a high premium, but one which is bad for society because of expected value-lost, then the director faces a quandry. He has to choose between what is good for his company's shareholders, accepting the offer, and what is good for society, rejecting the offer. In most western societies this is perhaps easily resolved: the law requires a director to promote the interests of the company shareholders, even when society is thereby disadvantaged. It is primarily the directors of the buying company that must bear the responsibility for hurting society (and their own shareholders) in such an unfortunate situation. The fear here is that a director may be tempted to rationalize the rejection of an unwanted but attractive takeover bid as not being in the interests of society.

The Spin-Off Situation

The decision rule for spin-offs was:

SPIN-OFF IF THE COSTS OF BEING A PART OF THE PARENT EXCEED THE BENEFITS AND A DESIRABLE SALE CANNOT BE ARRANGED.

In this circumstance, what is good for shareholders is clearly also good for society. When you consider that a company which self-atomizes into its various components will reduce any chance of abusive market power and of objectionable concentrated control, then the value to society of a split-up of the company will be even greater than it would be to the shareholders. If anything, it is in society's interests to promote spin-offs.

To summarize, in a buying situation a director need not be concerned with the impact on society because while the value-added may be marginally greater to a company's shareholders, the criterion is more stringent. In the selling situation, there could well be a conflict between what is good for the company's shareholders and what is good for society in the particular situation where the buying company is seeking an unfortunate acquisition, in which there is value-lost. In the spin-off situation, what is good for shareholders is even better for society, and the director would be advised to encourage any attempts to split up a company into its various components.

Notes

[1] Joel M. Stern, "Market Efficiency Varies" in *Analytical Methods in Financial Planning*, 2d ed. Booklet published by The Chase Manhattan Bank, New York, 1974.

[2] An overview of the studies is provided by Eugene F. Fama in "Efficient Capital Markets: A Review of Theory and Empirical Work," *The Journal of Finance*, May 1970.

[3] For an overview, refer to Buzzell, Gale, and Sultan "Market Share—A Key to Profitability," *Harvard Business Review*, January-February 1975.

[4] See note 3.

[5] Joel Dean and Winfield Smith, "The Relationship between Profitability and Size," in *The Corporate Merger*, ed. William W. Alberts and Joel E. Segall (Chicago: University of Chicago Press, 1966 and 1974).

[6] D. G. McFetridge and L. J. Weatherley, "Notes on the Economies of Large Firm Size," Royal Commission on Corporate Concentration, Study No. 20, (Minister of Supply and Services, Canada), Sections 3-2-3, 3-2-4, 3-2-5.

[7] Consider the following situation: A company has $100 of debt plus $150 of equity to give $250 of total capital. It is earning 15 percent after tax per year on its total capital, $37.50. It sells for an average P/E ratio of eight, to give a market value of $300. The company now reduces the cost of its debt by two percent, saving $2 in interest payments and increasing its aftertax earnings by $1. Thus it is now earning $38.50. At the P/E ratio of eight, it is now worth $308, a 2.67 percent increase.

[8] Shannon Pratt, "Valuing a Business," (Dow Jones-Irwin, 1981) Chapter 10.

[9] Report of the Royal Commission on Corporate Concentration, March 1978, Minister of Supply and Services, Canada, p. 66 and p. 115.

[10] Shyam Sunder, "An Empirical Study of Stock Price and Risk as They Relate to Accounting Changes in Inventory Valuation Methods," unpublished doctoral thesis, University of Chicago. This paper observed an increase in market value in the year in which a firm changed from FIFO to LIFO. However, because companies may tend to make this switch in a "good" year, Sunder could not conclude that all (or any) of the observed increase in market value was due to the switch to LIFO.

[11] "Technological Innovation: Its Environment and Management," U.S. Department of Commerce, January 1967.

[12] "Corporate Execs Often Lost in Shuffle After Acquisition," *Chicago Tribune,* October 24, 1979.

[13] "The Merger Boom Breeds More Insider Trading," *Business Week,* November 5, 1979.

[14] "The Game Isn't Over," *Business Week,* February 5, 1979.

[15] Report of the Royal Commission on Corporate Concentration, p. 120.

[16] "Return of the Octopus," the *Economist,* May 29, 1976.

[17] Interview with Franco Modigliani, reported in an article titled "The Case for an Undervalued Stock Market," *Business Week,* November 3, 1980.

[18] Richard P. Rumelt, *Strategy, Structure and Economic Performance* (Cambridge, Mass.: Harvard University Press, 1974).

[19] Report of the Royal Commission on Corporate Concentration, March 1978, Minister of Supply Services Canada, Table 5-11, p. 117.

[20] R. Hal Mason and Maurice B. Goudswaard, "Performance of Conglomerate Firms," *The Journal of Finance,* March 1976.

[21] Royal Commission on Corporate Concentration, Table 5-10, p. 117.

[22] Royal Commission on Corporate Concentration, p. 132.

[23] See note 8.

[24] See note 10.

[25] "The Cash-Flow Takeover Formula," *Business Week,* December 18, 1978.

[26] "General Electric's Very Personal Merger," *Fortune,* August 1977.

[27] "Break Up Big Oil?" *Forbes,* July 20, 1981.

[28] "Smaller is Beautiful for Britain's Giant GEC," the *Economist,* February 9, 1980.

[29] "The Spin-Off Gambit," *Forbes,* November 12, 1979.

[30] Interview titled "What's in It for Du Pont" in the article "The Making of the Megamerger," *Fortune,* September 7, 1981.

[31] "Du Pont Holders Approve Merger with Conoco Inc.," *The Wall Street Journal,* August 18, 1981.

[32] The Report of the Royal Commission on Corporate Concentration found that the 27.3 percent price

premium paid on average by the conglomerates they studied accounted for 2.7 of the 3.3 percent difference in returns to shareholders of conglomerates and of portfolios. (Table 5-10, page 117. Conglomerates returned 9.4 percent, portfolios returned 12.7 percent, 3.3 percent more. However, portfolios when penalized for the 27.3 percent premium returned 10 percent, still .6 percent more than the conglomerates.) The remaining .6 percent difference is due to the additional operational costs of conglomerates, and to the multibusiness discount. If it was all due to the discount, this would point to a 6 percent reduction in values. This is an upper limit. The actual reduction would be less because operational costs do exist and can be significant.

[33] "In the Battle for Conoco, Takeover Speculators Can Do Little More Than Watch the Action," *The Wall Street Journal*, July 31, 1981.

[34] "The Making of the Megamerger," *Fortune*, September 7, 1981.

[35] See note 31.

[36] "Du Pont Co. Agrees to Buy Conoco Inc. for Cash, Stock Totaling $6.82 Billion," *The Wall Street Journal*, July 7, 1981.

[37] "Du Pont's Costly Bet on Conoco," *Business Week*, July 20, 1981.

[38] See note 37.

[39] See note 31.

[40] The reported earnings will actually drop by $50 million. As discussed in Section I in the section on taxation benefits, the share price will actually rise because of the reduction in taxes paid (des-

pite the drop in reported earnings) in a sophisticated market. Du Pont's market, the New York Stock Exchange, is sophisticated. This rise is because a corporation will be actually keeping more, that is, earning more. Hence the use of "real" earnings, as distinguished with "reported" or "accounting" earnings.

[41] See note 30.

[42] See note 36.

[43] See note 32.

[44] "Exxon's Earnings Increase by 77%, Conoco's 317%" *The Wall Street Journal*, July 23, 1981.

[45] "The Blue Chips: Betting on Diversity," *Mainliner Magazine,* March 1977.

[46] See page 130.

Note: A seminal paper that was not referred to directly, but which had considerable influence on the author, is "The Profitability of Growth by Merger" by William W. Alberts, in *The Corporate Merger,* ed. William W. Alberts and Joel E. Segall (Chicago: University of Chicago Press, 1966 and 1974), p. 235.

At 38.28 per share, the premium to the Conoco shareholders was:

	($ millions)
Price paid—cash for 39 million shares at 98 plus 82 million Du Pont shares at 38.28	$6,961
Stand-alone value—87 million Conoco shares at 50	4,350
Premium	$2,611

The source of this premium was:

3 percent revaluation of Conoco for the breakup and hence elimination of the multibusiness discount	$ 131
The value-added—(see Table 2)	1,217
Transfer of wealth from the Du Pont shareholders to the Conoco shareholders—156 million Du Pont shares times the reduction from 46⅜ to 38.28	1,263
	$2,611

If the Du Pont shares do fall to 35, then the premium to the Conoco shareholders will fall to:

Premium at 38.28	$2,611
Anticipation of future "bloodlettings"—82 million Du Pont shares owned by the Conoco shareholders times the reduction from 38.28 to 35	269
Premium at 35	$2,342

	($ millions)
The loss to the Du Pont shareholders at 35 will be:	
Transferred to the Conoco shareholders—(see above)....................	$1,263
Anticipation of future "bloodlettings"—156 million shares times the further reduction from 38.28 to 35	512
	$1,775

Index

A

Anticipatory price rise of takeover target; *see also* Insider trading *and* Market value
  average values, 34
  causes of, 9, 34, 68-69
  correction for, 34, 35
  in Du Pont/Conoco merger, 92
  Poseidon, 5-6
Antitrust considerations, 39-40, 102, 108, 115-116, 120
Avis, 52

B

Bargains, 48-53
  1 in sophisticated markets, 48-49
  2 multibusinesses, 49-50
  3 conglomerates, 49-50
  4 in unsophisticated markets, 49-51
  5 contrary investments, 50
  6 in inflationary environments, 50-51
  7 closely held companies, 51-53
  8 negotiation, 51
  9 diversifiers, 51
  10 cash needy, 51-52
  11 time pressured, 52
  12 problem child, 52
  13 indicated by book value, 53
  definition of, 48
  to enable diversification, 55
  evaluation of, 34-35
  strategy, pursuit of, 48-53
  validation of/capitalizing on, 35, 48-49
Beatrice Foods, 51, 107, 108, 117
Benefits (*see* Operational *or* Nonoperational benefits)
Braun, Fred, 70
Browning-Ferris, 40

Business Development Services Inc., 56
Buy decision point
  criterion, 33
  society's perspective and criterion, 119-120
  step 1—estimate offered price, 33-34, 89-90
  step 2—estimate seller's stand-alone value, 34-35, 90-93
  step 3—determine price premium, 35-36, 93
  step 4—estimate value-added, 36, 93-99
  step 5—compare premium to value-added, 36, 99
  tabulation of steps for Du Pont/Conoco, 100
Buy strategies
  pursuit of bargains, 48-53
  pursuit of value-added, 37-48
Buyer results
  large companies, 108-109
  lose, 107-108
  lose/lose, 108
  small companies, 108
  win, 107
  win/win, 107

C

Capital structure, effect of, 21-22
Carborundum, 76
Catalyst, to enable diversification, 54
Chrysler Corporation, 12, 71
Cities Service, 88
Closely held companies
  as bargains, 51-52
  need to diversify, 24, 46, 51
Codex Corporation, 13, 107
Colgate-Palmolive, 27, 28, 81-82, 108
Competitive and market power, 115-116

Concentrated control, 116-117
Conglomerate acquisitions
  arguments in defence of, 61-63
  bar graph of performance shortfall, 62
  as bargains, 49-50
  empirical evidence on performance, 59-61
  general discussion of strategy, 40-43
  strategy path, 59
Conoco
  selling director's decision process, 99-102
  selling shareholder's decision process, 105
  takeover by Du Pont, 87-107, 108
Contrary investment strategy, 50
Cost of capital
  debt vs. equity, 21-22
  effect of a public or freer market, 17, 18
  general discussion of, 17-18
  RCCC studies, 17
Costs and production benefits; *see also* Value-added
  description, 12
  in conglomerate acquisitions, 41
  in Du Pont/Conoco merger, 94-95
  in horizontal acquisitions, 38
Costs in an acquisition
  1 front-end, 25, 38-39, 42, 97-98
  2 direct ongoing, 25-26, 38-39, 42, 98
  3 managerial, 26-27, 38-39, 42, 98
  4 learning, 27-28, 39, 42, 98
  5 opportunity, 28-29, 39, 42, 98
  6 multibusiness discount, 29, 39, 42, 98
  general method to value, 91-92
Countercyclical businesses, 13, 54
Country customs, effect on market sophistication, 8, 92
Country development, effect on market sophistication, 8, 92
Criteria; *see* Decision criteria
Crutcher Resources, Corp., 14

D

Dannon Yogurt, 117
Decision criteria for companies
  buying, 33
  selling, 67
  spinning-off, 80
Decision criteria for society
  buying, 119-120
  selling, 120-121

Decision criteria for society—*Cont.*
  spinning-off, 121
Del Monte, 28, 76
Depletion allowance, 22, 96-97
Depreciation expense, 22
Direct ongoing costs; *see also* Value-added
  in conglomerate acquisitions, 42
  description of, 25-26
  in Du Pont/Conoco merger, 98
  in horizontal acquisitions, 38-39
Discount
  integrated companies, 80
  for multibusinesses, 29, 91
  for nonmarketability, 18, 67-68
Dislocations and unemployment, 117-118
Diversification
  closely held companies, 24, 46, 51
  general discussion of, 23-24
  public companies, 24
Diversifying successfully, strategies for
  1 international ventures, 53
  2 resource commonalities, 53-54
  3 linked chain, 54
  4 catalyst, 54
  5 management expertise, 55
  6 nonoperational benefits, 55
  7 bargains, 55
  8 foothold/venture capitalist, 55-56
  9 holding company, to limit loss, 56
Dome Petroleum, 87, 92
Du Pont
  buying director's decision process, 89-99
  buying shareholder's decision process, 105-106
  takeover of Conoco, 87-107, 108
Due diligence
  necessity of when buying, 34
  necessity of when selling, 67, 101, 110

E

Earnings per share valuation, 72-75
Efficient markets; *see* Market sophistication *and* Sophisticated markets
Empirical evidence on strategies, 56-63
External information, effect on market sophistication, 5-6, 90-91
Exxon Corporation or Exxon Enterprises, 14, 54, 90

F

Fallacies (some prevalent ones)
  avoid taxes on dividends, 20-21

Fallacies—*Cont.*
   diversify for the shareholders, 23-24
   foreign companies are cheap, 70-71
   market value is price paid, 79
   open too high, 78
   pay a premium for control, 78-79
   sell for less than spin-off value, 81, 82
   share markets are unsophisticated, 71
   survive at any cost, 76-77
   use earnings per share to value, 72-75
Familial benefits; *see also* Value-added
   1 entree to closed business or country, 24-25
   2 local equity participation, 25
   to enable diversification, 55
   in Du Pont/Conoco merger, 97
Far-Mar-Co, 18
Farmland Industries, 18, 19
First Boston Corp., 106
Fleetwood Enterprises, 14, 54
Foothold/venture capitalist, to enable diversification, 55-56
Ford Motor, 12, 37-43
Front-end costs; *see also* Value-added
   in conglomerate acquisitions, 42
   description of, 25
   in Du Pont/Conoco merger, 97-98
   in horizontal acquisitions, 38-39
Funding benefits; *see also* Value-added
   1 ability to raise capital, 16-17
   2 cost of capital, 17-18
   3 ability to allocate capital, 18-19
   4 ability to do large projects, 19
   in Du Pont/Conoco merger, 96

G

Games
   "Cut the Capital Budget," 28
   bridge, 15, 26, 55
   fish, 15, 55
General Electric, 56, 78
General Electric Co. Ltd., The (of U.K.), 82
General Motors, 12, 40
Grace, W. R., 83

H

Hedge, natural resource, 97
Helena Rubinstein, 27, 28, 81-82, 108
Hollingsworth & Whitney, 13
Horizontal acquisitions
   empirical evidence on performance, 59
   general discussion of strategy, 37-40

Horizontal acquisitions—*Cont.*
   graph of results, 60
   strategy path, 59
Horizontal linked strategy
   description, 59
   empirical evidence on performance, 59
   to enable diversification (linked chain), 54
   graph of results, 60
   strategy path, 59
Howard Johnson, 11
Hudson Bay Oil and Gas, 87-88, 92-93

I

IBM, 83
Inflation
   as cause of bargains, 50-51
   effect on inventory valuation, 22, 71-72
Information policy, effect on market sophistication, 5, 90
Insider trading; *see also* Anticipatory price rise
   in Du Pont/Conoco merger, 92
   effect of, 9
   Poseidon, 5
Inventory valuation
   LIFO/FIFO, 71
   effect on market value, 22
ITT, 52

J

Jamieson, J. Kenneth, 14
Jefferson, Edward G., 90, 91, 94-95, 96, 97, 103
Joint ventures, 47-48
   diagram of, 49
   to enable diversification, 53
Jones, Reginald, 78

K-L

Kennecott Copper, 76
Learning costs; *see also* Value-added
   in conglomerate acquisitions, 42
   description of, 27-28
   in Du Pont/Conoco merger, 98
   in horizontal acquisitions, 39
Leveraged buyouts, 21
Linked chain; *see* Horizontal linked strategy

M

Malaysian cement market, 7

Managerial benefits; *see also* Value-added
  in conglomerate acquisitions, 41-42
  description of, 14-15
  in Du Pont/Conoco merger, 96
  to enable diversification, 55
  in horizontal acquisitions, 38
Managerial costs; *see also* Value-added
  in conglomerate acquisitions, 42
  description of, 26-27
  in Du Pont/Conoco merger, 98
  in horizontal acquisitions, 38-39
Market size, effect on market sophistication, 8, 92
Market sophistication; *see also* Sophisticated markets
  characteristics of a perfect market, 4
  classes/degrees of, 8-10
  factors influencing, 4-8, 90-92
  graphs of responsiveness, 10
Market value
  definition of, 4
  estimating buyer's postacquisition value, 3, 103, 104
  estimating seller's preacquisition value, 34-35, 68-69
  factors influencing, 113-114
  maximization, appropriateness of, 113-114
  postannouncement drop in buyer's value, 106
  rise in seller's value in anticipation of takeover, 34, 68-69
  table to estimate Du Pont's, 104
Mead Corporation, 77
Milliken, Frank, 76
Mobil Oil, 88, 102
Monopoly power, 115-116
Motorola Inc., 12-13, 107
Multibusiness
  as bargains, 49-50
  effect on market sophistication, 6, 91
Multibusiness discount costs; *see also* Value-added
  in conglomerate acquisitions, 42
  description of, 29
  in Du Pont/Conoco merger, 98
  estimation of, 127-128
  in horizontal acquisitions, 39
Multiple classifications study
  1 single business, 57
  2 constrained-dominant, 57
  3 constrained-related, 57-58
  4 linked-dominant, 58
  5 linked-related, 58
  6 vertical-dominant, 58

Multiple classifications study—*Cont.*
  7 unrelated-dominant, 58
  8 unrelated businesses, 59
  graphs of results, 60
  strategy paths, 59

N

New York Stock Exchange; *see* Stock exchanges
Nonmarketability discount, 18, 67-68
Nonoperational benefits; *see also* Value-added
  1 funding, 16-20, 96
  2 taxes, 20-22, 96-97
  3 risk, 23-24, 97
  4 familial, 24-25, 97
  to enable diversification, 43, 55
  inability to guide normal strategy formulation, 38
Northwest Industries, 72

O

Oasis chain of restaurants, 11
Operational benefits; *see also* Value-added
  1 sales and marketing, 11-12, 37, 41, 94
  2 costs and production, 12, 38, 41, 94-95
  3 research and technology, 12-13, 38, 41, 95
  4 resource, 13-14, 38, 41, 96
  5 managerial, 14-15, 38, 41-42, 96
  general method to value, 93-94
  realization of, 15-16, 36
Opportunity costs; *see also* Value-added
  in conglomerate acquisitions, 42
  description of, 28-29
  in Du Pont/Conoco merger, 98
  in horizontal acquisitions, 39

P

Peabody Coal, 76
Peabody International, 70
Philip Morris, 28
Popularity, effect on market sophistication, 6, 91-92
Portfolio concepts
  cash generators and cash users, 20-21, 75
  of diversified businesses, 23-24
  wildcats, stars, cows, dogs, 6, 77-78
Poseidon, 5

Predatory pricing, 116
Premium
  average values, 35-36
  calculation of, 33-35, 67-69
  for control, 78-79
  decay in, 69, 102, 105, 130-131
  definition of, 33
  in Du Pont/Conoco merger, 93, 105
Proctor & Gamble, 28
Purchasing power, 116

R

R. J. Reynolds, 28-29, 76
Rasmussen, Wallace N., 117
Research and technology benefits; *see also* Value-added
  description of, 12-13
  in conglomerate acquisitions, 41
  in Du Pont/Conoco merger, 95
  in horizontal acquisitions, 38
Resource benefits; *see also* Value-added
  description of, 13-14
  in conglomerate acquisitions, 41
  in Du Pont/Conoco merger, 96
  to enable diversification, 53-54
  in horizontal acquisitions, 38
Risk benefits; *see also* Value-added
  1 ability to do risky projects, 23
  2 diversification, 23-24
  in Du Pont/Conoco merger, 97
Rumsfeld, Donald, 5

S

Sales and marketing benefits; *see also* Value-added
  in conglomerate acquisitions, 41
  description of, 11-12
  in Du Pont/Conoco merger, 94
  in horizontal acquisitions, 37
Scott Paper, 13
Sea-Land Service Inc., 28, 76
Seagram, 88
Searle, G. D., & Co., 5, 52
Security analyst's evaluation
  general method of, 102-105
  tabulation of steps for Du Pont/Conoco, 104
Sell decision point
  criterion, 67
  society's perspective and criterion, 120-121
  step 1—estimate offered price, 67-68, 99-101
  step 2—estimate seller's stand-alone value, 68-69, 101

Sell decision point—*Cont.*
  step 3—determine if premium positive, 69, 101
  step 4—judge if best offer, 69, 101-102
Sell strategies
  pursuit of logical buyer, 70
  pursuit of sugar daddies, 70-79
Seller results; *see also* Premium, 109-110
Shareholder following, effect on market sophistication, 7, 92
Shearson Loeb Rhodes Inc., 52, 107
Society
  benefits to, 3, 114-115
  costs to, 115
  interest in, 113-119
Sophisticated markets; *see also* Market sophistication
  chance of finding a bargain in, 48
  description of a perfect market, 4
  reported vs. real earnings, 22, 71, 97, 128-129
Spin-off decision point
  criterion, 80
  society's perspective and criterion, 121
Spin-off strategy, 80-83
Stand-alone value of a company
  of Conoco, 90-93
  general discussion of, 4-10
  method to estimate, 34-35, 68-69
Stock exchanges
  Calcutta, 9
  Indonesia, 8
  London, 8, 9
  Melbourne, 9
  New York, 8-10, 89, 92
  Sydney, 9
  Tokyo, 9
Strategic implications of an acquisition, 103-104
Strategy paths
  1 horizontal strategy, 59
  2 linked horizontal strategy, 59
  3 vertical strategy, 59
  4 conglomerate strategy, 59
  graphs of performance, 60
Strengths and weaknesses, matching of, 46-47
Sugar daddies
  1 foreigners, 70-71
  2 superior judges of worth, 71-72
  3 earnings per share boosters, 72-75
  4 highly leveraged, 75
  5 cash rich, 75-76
  6 shrinking/failing company, 76-77
  7 wildcat and star worshippers, 77-78

Sugar daddies—*Cont.*
  8 monument builders, 78
  9 investment banker clients, 78-79
  strategy, pursuit of, 70-79

T

Tax benefits; *see also* Value-added
  1 write-off of losses, 20
  2 avoidance of tax on dividends, 20-21
  3 capital structure, 21-22
  4 depreciation/depletion expenses, 22
  5 inventory valuation, 22
  in DuPont/Conoco merger, 96-97
  to enable diversification, 55
  society's view, 118-119
Tec Tank, 70
Trading activity, effect on market sophistication, 7, 92
Treasury stock, purchase of, 20-21

U-W

U.S. Life, 40
Utah International, 56, 78

Validation of high price/bargain, 35, 48-49, 79
Valuation; *see also* Market value
  of stand-alone company, 34-35, 68-69
  of value-added, 93-94
Value-added
  definitions of, 10-11
  general discussion of, 10-29
  general method to value, 93-94
  market acceptance requirement, 18-19
  realization of, 15-16, 36
  to society, 119-120
  strategy, pursuit of, 37-48
Value-added and relatedness
  general discussion of, 43-46
  graphs, 45
Venture capitalist/foothold, to enable diversification, 55-56
Vertical acquisitions
  empirical evidence on performance, 59
  general discussion of strategy, 43
  graph of results, 60
  strategy path, 59

Waste Management, 40
Weinstock, Sir Arnold, 82